CW00525678

NO BEER ON A DEAD PLANET

NO BEER ON A DEAD PLANET

Jono Coote

Red Fez Books

First published in 2021 by Red Fez Books

Copyright 2021 Jono Coote

ISBN: 978-1-8383421-0-4

Typeset and designed by Josh Sutton in Garamond and EB Garamond

Cover design & illustration by Red Fez Books

Chapter illustrations by Lewis Brownlie (www.lewisbrownlie.com)

Printed and bound by the Gutenberg Press, Malta

CONTENTS

Acknowledgement

I acknowledge the traditional custodians of the land in which this book is set (particularly the Wurundjeri Woi-wurrung people of the Kulin Nations, where the majority of my time was spent), and recognise their continuing connection to the land, water and community. I pay respects to the Elders past, present and emerging, and extend that respect to all Aboriginal and Torres Strait Islander peoples.

"Despair is the armchair; its indifference and glazed, incurious eyes. I think travellers are essentially optimists, or else they would never go anywhere ."

Paul Theroux, *The Old Patagonian Express*

"For me, skating and travelling are fucking the same thing..."

"Every time you picked up a board, that's what skating's been – it's taken you a little bit further from your house every day you did it. This is just an extension of when we first stepped on a board, this is how far we've gone now."

Excerpt from Antihero Skateboards' Australian tour video *Tent City*

CHAPTER ONE

The lager soy cocktail

"You can try some – I don't mind, we can share," said our host magnanimously. The drink he spoke of sat beside us, swarming neon of Taipei's night glinting from the bottle's side, the half drunk contents, the ominously floating flakes like drifts of dandruff preserved in alcohol. I began travelling for adventure, to discover cultural quirks, to try new things – but it's only day three and I may have already found my threshold. Lager, traditionally, is not a drink which is known for its mixing qualities beyond a little lemonade now and then. It has been many things to many people; it has started and ended lifelong friendships, it has caused wars; it has sparked brilliant ideas, it drives an industry employing millions, it has killed, it has been the nucleus which nurtures emotional rebirth. It has not, as far as I am aware, gained popularity as the perfect accompaniment to warm soy milk, but this is the drink which sits before me now.

Skateboarders as a group have a habit of letting their egos allow themselves the extravagance of seeing themselves as the alpha traveller, immediately meeting up with locals upon reaching their destination and heading to obscure suburbs rather than tourist hotspots. Entering the social milieu at a level way beyond that of the 'Five Countries in Five Days' package tour groups, determined to fit as many Instagram 'moments' as they can, is a subtle stroke of the collective ego. The truth is, however, that for the most part McDonald's dinners and cheap off license beers buttressed with chronic (the traditional skate trip purchase most supportive of local entrepreneurs) are the standard. Local culture beyond the level of skateboarding can (and I'm making a sweeping exaggeration here) be heavily overlooked. This is no more noticeable than when you step off the plane and into a city without an immediately notable skate scene, or a point of contact to ease you into said scene. During our first two days in Taipei I saw no more than one skateboarder on the streets, wildly mongo pushing his way to some unknown destination and with giant headphones jammed on to block out any potential human interaction. Without the usual immediate contact with local skaters I was forced into exploration beyond that which results in frontside grinds, but it's no bad thing having a few days away from slamming on concrete and my limbs weren't too put out at the down time. Hashtag #skateeverydamnday is fine if you're an intellectually challenged social media addict, or a swoosh rider who has to use it otherwise their per diem will be cut (alongside being dragged away from family and friends and sent to work on sewing shoes by hand in an export processing zone); but for the rest of us, it's probably best to skate when you want to and, just perhaps, expand your interests in between those periods of relentless mobbed kickflips and early grabbed stinkbug airs. Even if your other interests consist of boozing your bleary-eyed way across continents, the switch up will still enrich your life in some way. I guarantee it.

The previous winter in London had been a long, arduous slog of damp walks, sheltering in overpriced pubs, cancelled trains and plans continuously pushed forward until some dimly imagined time when the sun would return. Dreams of escape from the drizzle-cloaked peaks and troughs of its skyline, intruding on my thoughts more and more with the passing of years, finally coalesced into flights booked and routes mapped out. When the time finally came to act upon these plans London lay below, rainswept and acquiescent to the elements which were buffeting our plane about the skies, the city a squat malevolent bullfrog crafted from steel and concrete and pierced with pinpricks of dull light from the windows of thousands of uniformly bleak office buildings. I dreamed of Antipodean ozone holes from my window seat. A year in Australia with my partner Alyce was to be the antidote to terminal smog psychosis, a very real issue which affects the majority of the UK capital's population in some way or another. Thoughts of endless sunshine, gently curving beaches, rainforest hikes and UV-enhanced skateparks had been bouncing through my mind ever since our flights were booked. Long ago, an especially eccentric RE teacher at my school was posited with the notion that maybe heaven and hell don't really exist – after all, the living haven't been there and returned to confirm its existence. "Well, you could say the same about Australia," was her immediate and confident reply. I considered this philosophical quandary as our flight thundered above the earth's surface but, having proved her wrong personally on a couple of occasions previously, I felt confident that my plane would arrive at a substantive destination.

I was also looking forward to checking the veracity of Australia as existing terra firma by putting urethane to every hardened surface I could find. Being a skateboarder has a habit of leading you to destinations unlikely to feature prominently in Lonely Planet guidebooks – from dodging broken glass and dog eggs in rough council estates in Madrid to searching for dry ditches in the Yorkshire hills, the places I've travelled to ride a four wheeled plank of wood form a map of almost farcical eclectica. Judging by the scathing insults heaped upon it by any number of Australians that I have mentioned the place to, it appears that skateboarders are some of the few people excited by the prospect of visiting Canberra, the nation's much maligned capital. The delights of the capital city, however, would have to wait until further down the road.

Taipei is a city which manages to incorporate the modern city's race to the skies without the all-too-hectic vibe which this can arouse; harried-looking businessmen unwind after a day in the office at the city's numerous night markets, welcoming residents offer up a taste of their dinner to passers by in the shadow of some of the world's most expensive hotels, thickly wooded hills peppered with Buddhist temples lie enticingly close to the Central Business District. We hiked up Elephant Mountain, explored the culinary delights of various night markets and drank more of the creatively named 'Taiwan Beer' than was strictly healthy in an attempt to get a grip on Taipei's beating heart.

Sloshing our way down from Elephant Mountain in a downpour, we stopped to buy a drink from an elderly couple's roadside stall and, beckoning us in, they invited us to share their meal with them. Sitting under a parasol, watching sheets of rain sweep across the city as we make conversation based around hand gestures and tuck into a pork broth washed down with thankfully soy milk-free lager, I muse on the unlikeliness of this happening in London's Square Mile; hospitality is clearly a cornerstone of the city's cultural make up.

A visit to the Taipei Museum of Contemporary Art saw us quickly reach the depths of discombobulation attempting to comprehend theoretical modern art concepts realised not just in another language, but in a completely different script. Haphazardly placed signs with English translations served only to offer up more questions than answers, and we don't last too long in there. These barriers mean we don't glean as much as I would like to from the museum's exhibitions, but the more decipherable artworks show a trope which seems to be cropping up repeatedly across cultures worldwide; a fear of the relentless march of technology and its effects on societal interactions. How this will affect the generosity and friendliness we received in Taiwan for future visitors will, I suppose, remain to be seen.

A skate mission on the last day is preceded the night before by a visit to a city centre skate shop (that social hub which is itself intrinsically threatened by the internet) to grab a skate tool, where a friendly shop lurker brings up the subject of the aforementioned lager soy cocktail. I can now safely say, if someone offers you a taste of this intriguingly revolting drink, you should make yourself scarce fast. Hops and soybeans roll around my stomach as our host guides us to what he says is the nearest bar district, which turns out to be overpriced hipster hell. Heading down to the lower level on his recommendation, ruinous drinks clutched in hand as if they were the precious gems that their price tag suggested, we find the room empty but for two people – a slightly built woman plinking away at the piano and singing "The time has come for Christmas cheer" in a high, wavering voice, and our man accompanying the seasonally unsuitable jingle with an out of time tapping on a small bongo drum. We make our excuses and leave, making our way to a night market via another pricey bar. The fiscal blow is softened by an entrance from the sales rep for a whiskey company and the fact that the friendly barman is willing to let me join in the testing, but it is clear that we aren't in an area suited to our means.

Taipei's extensive skatepark, however is, free. The clearly not too well looked after 13' vert ramp, with peeling Skatelite panels and protruding screws, isn't particularly appealing, but the rest of the park is kept in good condition. Clearly built more with bikes and blades than skateboards in mind, it still offers up plenty of fun once you look past the oversized jump boxes and triple kinked hubbas. Covered in sweat and dirt, stoked on the first roll of the trip, beers clutched firmly in hand, we are seen off by the city in glorious style that night on the banks of the Tamsui River. The sun makes its stately descent towards the horizon, streaks of red, gold and indigo trail in its wake and the rows of buildings across the opposite bank explode with light; shimmering reflections imprinted in the waters of the Tamsui River glowing like the gateway to a parallel universe. Four days is not enough time to fully appreciate Taipei itself, let alone the further reaches of Taiwan, and I am certain that we will be back.

CHAPTER TWO

Miserable Pommies and volcanic rims

In most countries, standing at the side of a busy road swinging a skateboard violently at local wildlife and shouting "I'll truck you, you cunt!" is a surefire way to gain firsthand experience of the hospitality offered by the local police force. In Australia however, during avian nesting season, people passing by will barely bat an eyelid. I know this from firsthand experience due to a close encounter with two mynah birds indulging in the peculiarly Australian practice of 'swooping' – Australian wildlife's homage to Alfred Hitchcock's *The Birds*, a psychotic extension of the parental instinct which sees magpies, mynah birds, crows and more, working themselves into a protective fury and aiming shrieking kamikaze swoops at any creature they deem a threat. Both me and the birds came away unscathed, but from that point onwards I stayed wary when skating the park local to our first Australian residence; Nundah's Flower Street Skatepark, a whippy bowled out miniramp with pool coping hidden deep in Brisbane's Northern suburbs. Other than time spent at Nundah Skatepark or dodging kamikaze birds, our first few days in Australia – as is generally the case when jet lagged to the point of existential insignificance – are not massively productive. Beers by the river, forays into the four block city centre and meeting up with the surprising amount of friends and acquaintances the two of us have scattered across the suburban sprawl helps acquaint us with the city's kinks and quirks. We slowly acclimatise to an intense and increasing heat which is strong enough to have mummified the bodies of geckos we find stuck to the front door of one of our residences, a reminder if ever one was needed to put on sun cream as we leave in the morning.

Days pass in a blur of thunderstorms and whiskey, sunset DIY spot missions, bombing hills and taking stock of the city's residents. Brisbane is a small city with the vibe and all the inherent eccentricities of a large outback town – something which makes people-watching a truly rewarding or terrifying experience, depending on your point of view. On our second day we find ourselves sat on the bus on the way to Brisbane's Southbank while a heavily muscled roid-freak does push ups at the front, and eye contact is studiously avoided by all. Later on, exploring the littered remnants of the 1988 World Expo preserved next to the river, a repetitive bellow echoes along the river, "They laugh at me, but won't face me in the ring. Who's going to put their fists up, BOSTON STYLE?! Haha, whhooooo!!!" He enters our field of vision from around a bend in the river, furiously shadowboxing as he chants, upright, proud, but somehow profoundly depressing – a ghost from Scorsese's cutting room floor, a twisted and strangely sad shadow of Hollywood archetype, proudly shouting his nonsense credo to thin air and the same downcast eyes appear on the faces of the tourists at the Nepalese Peace Pagoda as appeared earlier on the bus.

The storms really take hold as we head to the Gold Coast, called the South Coast until 1958 when it was renamed to reflect the rampant growth of the tourist industry along this southern stretch of Queensland's coastline. Small towns dotted along the beach were first connected, then swallowed whole, by holiday resorts, theme parks and casinos. Before long the developments spread all the way down to the New South Wales border like a rash, Australia's very own beefed up Newquay; surfers, stag and hen parties, musclebound v-neck t-shirt wearers heckling from the pavement, "Do a kickflip Tony Hawk!" and gaggles of tourists. We stay in hotels and with relatives, always a few suburbs removed from the epicentre of the chaos, managing to avoid Surfer's

Paradise comprehensively. Finding ourselves instead next to Pizzey Park comes as a particularly galling dose of salt in a wound as I look upon one of the world's most iconic and currently most rain lashed skateparks. Queensland in October doesn't always deliver the weather you would expect, so exploring ancient concrete relics of past skate cultures is pushed forward to some hoped-for future date.

Our accommodation for one week of this leg is run by a pair of heavily tanned and mustachioed brothers of Greek origin, who are furnished with the monikers Zeus and Poseidon. We never get around to asking whether those were the names given to them by their parents at birth. There is an air of low key criminality exuding from their whole enterprise which is perhaps confirmed when, early one morning, I respond to a knock on the door to find two police officers enquiring after a possible tenant. I send them on their way, and bring it up with Poseidon when he appears in the shared kitchen later that day as we make our lunch. His eyebrows raise in a theatrical caricature of disbelief; "Police ... round here?!? I have no idea what they might have wanted. I've never even heard of anyone of that name... Michael? Hey Zeus, do you know anyone named Michael?" He simultaneously titters, leers nervously at us and scans the room for a change of subject, until his eyes alight on our half-made sandwiches. "Jeez," he exclaims with feeling, "you guys must really like tomatoes."

The majority of our time is spent drinking, reading books, drinking, slogging through gale force winds and pelting rain in the name of 'getting some fresh air', and more drinking. The Gold Coast's charms are heavily geared towards the outdoors and, when these options aren't available, you might as well be in an East Sussex retirement town. Night time walks along deserted beaches may sound romantic, conjuring images of stolen moonlit kisses scored by the sibilant hiss of the tide, but consistent downpours and driving sand scouring any inch of exposed skin make for more endurance test than pleasant stroll.

Vitamin D chasing brings us to the Sunshine Coast, relishing the opportunity to stretch legs under blue skies and take advantage of the new park at Alexandra Heads to nearly dislocate my pelvis hanging up on a back smith – "Isaac Newton is a very good ghost.

One of the best," as stated by Robert M. Pirsig's ghost of Phaedrus, but sometimes I think he's probably just a cunt with a hard on for watching skateboarders slam. We're in the bar cutting through the serotonin with alcohol long before that evening's storm hits, laughing over beers from our window seats at what is a light drizzle compared to what we've experienced over the past week.

The Sunshine Coast is famed for its National Park hikes and the Glass House Mountains sit tantalisingly close. Like strange monuments to old gods, from our coastal view looking inland these monolithic rocks seem to erupt vertically from the surrounding plain, electric with the promise of hidden secrets left by ancient civilizations. The sight of them awakens a primal urge to explore, but, hamstrung by our lack of vehicle, they merely form a backdrop to our train journeys up and down this stretch of Queensland and our experience is mostly limited to the beaches and bars which make up a small stretch of the coastline around the seemingly idyllic retirement village of Caloundra. The sun shines, a thunderstorm rushing across the bay is an excuse to hit the bars, I pass by hundreds of op shops (Australian for charity shop), I see a young man sitting cross legged playing chess with a homeless man in the shade from an awning. One night on the way home from the pub we see four pasty, unhealthy looking office workers taking turns at slapping each other on a street corner, ill-lit by faulty street lights; but three days is not enough time to explore the dark underbelly, even of a town of this humble size, so we cast our eyes downward and walk on.

Heading back to Brisbane on Friday night, we almost immediately fall foul of Australia's totalitarian drinking laws when we attempt to go to see some punk bands with Alyce on a provisional UK Driver's License. The high tech scanning system which assists the bouncer, and which wouldn't look out of place in airport security, quickly decides that her ID doesn't exist and she definitely shouldn't be allowed into the venue. This doesn't mean I get back my own entry fee, of course, so we slope around the corner to a more welcoming bar 15 dollars worse off. The fact that happy hour is on makes me feel better, but the house band covering the likes of Wheatus and The Killers does not. It turns out that bands like this are the bread and butter of the Friday/Saturday night bar scene across the country, where non-discerning punters come to drink and dance to songs – which were terrible in the first place – somehow being butchered even further. A few days later, during a break from the session at Pizzey, my disdain for this kind of entertainment comes up in conversation. One of the skaters, more than a few beers deep, is truly aghast at the fact that I don't appreciate this as a backdrop to my drinking; letting me know in no uncertain terms that I'm a "miserable pommie cunt', which in the given circumstances is a badge I'm happy to wear with pride.

Livers suitably primed and ears unsuitably assaulted, we call it a night early. The next day is Rochdale Wizard Garry Giomarelli's leaving skate/piss-up at a backyard miniramp in the city's suburbs. As befits someone who once tried to convince me to eat steak he'd cut from a fox found dead at the side of the road, he has slotted in well within the scene of a state famed for both the rugged individualism and the eccentricity of its residents. Of course, the skateboarding magic which affords him his nickname and his willingness to chip in on a DIY spot build don't hurt. Neither me nor Garry are feeling particularly fresh when we meet up, so before joining the party we stop off at a sun-drenched DIY spot which is both the perfect warm up and hangover cure. We are joined hesitantly by some teenagers new to skateboarding and impart semi-incoherent wisdom upon the arts of ollieing and dutch courage before driving out to the house party, getting there late in the afternoon to find most of the crowd well on the way to sloppy drunk and relishing every minute of it. A session gets going with the dwindling number of sober skaters and, once everyone's figured out the ramp's kinks and quirks (and the suitability of their blood alcohol levels towards skateboarding), then it gets a seeing-to until nearly dark when the drinking can begin in earnest. Of course for most people it began long ago; so by the time we are done skating the majority of party goers are trolleyed, and by the time I'm half cut then the projectile vomiting has reached near Exorcist level proportions. The sensation of being within the splatter radius of a particularly powerful regurgitation can't really be put into words, but these things should be accepted with equanimity and I go wash the bigger chunks from the backs of my calves before cracking another beer.

The Gold Coast welcomes us back with another torrential downpour, which we watch approach Armageddon-like from the garden of a German beer hall in Brisbane, before leaving in an attempt to outrun it down the coast. Lightning cuts ominously through slate grey clouds, looming large in a way which is rarely seen in the UK – there's no doubt about it, Australia can lay on some impressive weather when it wants to. It also helps distract you from the fact that you're trying to recover from what is basically alcohol poisoning by introducing even more alcohol to your body. The weather passes after a day or two, leaving the Coast happily indulgent of our thirst for skateparks, beaches and hikes through verdant Australian bushland; all needs which went unfulfilled the first time around. Salk Oval melds different eras of skatepark design with guerilla 'crete flourishes, pool coping miniramps are found in quiet corners of football pitches and secret quarters lay dangerously close to ocean inlets.

Pizzey Skatepark, the centrepoint of the Gold Coast's glut of skateparks, is the stuff of legend. The park is the namesake of Jack Pizzey, former Queensland Premier and at the time of writing the most recent Australian head of state to die on duty. Death on duty is something which seems all too possible the first time you lay eyes on the park's original bowl, built in the 1980s by a swimming pool builder and featuring treacherously kinked transitions and a weathered concrete lip which elbows around before a steep descent towards a jarringly peaceful looking lake.

Large fruit bats hang en masse from tree branches sprawling over meandering bodies of water and large mansions sprawl towards the water's edge, giving some idea of the area's affluence. There is clearly money here, which alongside the deeply ingrained surf culture goes a long way towards explaining the volume and quality of skateparks to be found. In fact, this plethora of concrete in a way worked against me; my lack of connections within the local scene meant that I often found myself with huge skateparks all to myself for entire days. The lack of scooter kids was a definite plus, but a few fellow skaters to fire up the session definitely wouldn't have gone amiss.

One sunny afternoon we head out to Purling Brook Falls in Springbrook National Park, part of the ancient Gondwana Rainforests which stretch from Brisbane to Newcastle and which, in this area, form part of the rim of the crumbling Mount Warning caldera. We move slowly through these venerable life forms, with the sun occasionally shafting through the canopy before exploding in colour as the ground drops away at the various lookouts offering spectacular views of the range. The experience brings on something like the hush a tourist feels they must obey when entering a famous cathedral and it is only fitting that the site of a plastic bottle or wrapper, left by a careless sightseer, can bring on the kind of religious wrath which has you wishing a plague of boils upon the perpetrator. Unsurprisingly, the area abounds with the Creation Myths and Dreamtime Stories which make up an integral part of Aboriginal culture across Australia. The nearby twin peaks of Mount Cougal are named 'Ningeroongun' and 'Barrajanda' after the two hunting dogs of a renowned hunter, Gwyala. After being killed by a neighbouring tribe during a hunt, the dogs were each buried beneath a peak and so they have been known henceforth. The neighbouring tribe, meanwhile, were subject to a rainmaking ceremony which saw them buried beneath heavy landslides that forever altered the surrounding topography. These stories can be found across the entire continent, passed on by word of mouth through myriad generations. They demonstrate, through their close adherence to the geography they relate to, the indigenous Australian people's close connection with the land they have inhabited for thousands of years. Such naturally awe-inspiring surroundings make these tales seem particularly tangible. This is our first proper look at what wonders the Australian hinterlands have to offer, an all encompassing riot of greens and browns brought alive by the occasional glimpse of its denizens; lizards basking in dappled sunlight, bush turkeys crashing their awkward way through the undergrowth, termites exposed by an upturned piece of bark which traditionally formed a part of the local indigenous diet and taste like lively, squirming chunks of black pepper. The falls themselves are one of those strange tricks of nature where a seemingly calm pool suddenly reaches a sheer drop and finds itself crashing 300 feet down into the rainforest depths while incredible, undulating vistas free of any sign of the hand of man stretch far beyond the horizon. The coastal highway beckons, but the walks which have been laid out around this natural wonder see us out of Queensland in style.

One of the major news stories being picked apart when we decide to check back in with the world outside of our trip that night – apart from the usual political manoeuvring, American mass shootings and Donald Trump – surrounds the Australian cricket team being caught cheating in South Africa by sandpapering their balls (insert Viz character Finbarr Saunders cartoon here). A clearly well regarded Aussie cricketer is called in to discuss the matter and how heartbroken Australian cricket fans can be brought back into games, and his answer demands nothing less than extreme measures; "Put on free games, offer them free beer, whatever it takes!" This is clearly an issue of biblical proportions. Suitably caught up with the world's major issues, we decide to remove ourselves from the coverage of such shocking scenes and into New South Wales where our plans of media-free camping would make tales of cricket-based devilry harder to come by.

CHAPTER THREE

Watch out for the weird cunts

The Northern tip of New South Wales is not quite as well off as its neighbour to the North, something immediately apparent from the change in road quality as you cross the border. Much of the NSW stretch of the Pacific Highway which runs down the length of Australia's East Coast is undergoing a massive and necessary refurbishment but, away from the highway, dodging gaping potholes becomes a major tool in helping to stay alert when driving long distances. This dilapidation is perhaps in direct contradiction to its surrounding natural beauty, perhaps just an admission by those who live here that concrete and tarmac has no chance against the stunningly verdant backdrops we find ourselves travelling through. Far from the arid depictions of the Australia of popular myth, the northern New South Wales coast is as lush as the Valleys from which it takes its name. Byron Bay is the first stop after Queensland, a small, elegantly laid out town with a well off, middle-aged hippy vibe permeating the air – while the surrounding roads might not scream of investment, this place certainly does. Tourism is clearly king here and there is more incense than cheap hash in the air, but it nonetheless retains some of the laid back vibe for which it is famous. Our first NSW beers are soundtracked by live blues rock, courtesy of a talented guitarist and a clearly less gifted cohort trying to figure out how to play the drums, at the Beach Hotel which dominates the corner between the main strip and the beach. A warm wind drifts through the windows, bringing with it an ocean tang, and the booze isn't so pricey that we feel bad about staying for more than a few. On our way back to the campsite, bellies full of booze, a young drunk stops us with a mumbled tale of a hurt knee. On closer enquiry, however, he proves to just be incredibly pissed; the kind you can only reach with the assistance of a variety of strong liquors. We start to move on when he lurches to his feet and shouts "Wait! Do you know where the brewery is?" We don't, which elicits a pitying glance and the statement, "Well, you've gotten lucky. I'm the only nice bloke in New South Wales. The thing is" – and he leans in closely here to add gravity to his words – "the thing is, around here, you've got to watch out for the weird cunts." With that wisdom imparted, and with the visiting tourists now suitably warned, he meanders off down the street and into the warm Byron night.

The next day I decide to check out the town's only nod to skateboarders, a 1980s relic and certified oddity which some friends who we'd unexpectedly met up with on our entry to the campsite had warned would offer nothing but disappointment. As it turns out, the cracked concrete dish which I find is so ridiculous that I can't fail to have a good time; a bowled out flatbank made from near gravel, with a run-up consisting of a detour from the main footpath and a Lilliputian jump box. It was unlikely to host Street League anytime soon, but if you're not too picky (and I'm not) then fun could definitely be had. Halfway through the session we encounter a casualty of the area's hippy credentials – a sunburned, nervy shell of a man dressed in a biblical style robe with a dreadlock wig of the fancy dress shop variety poking out from under its hood. He tells Alyce to get off of her phone "before it atomises her" and then stumbles on past the skatepark, occasionally screaming at us, the trees or something visible only to him, to leave him alone. Watch out for the weird cunts indeed...

Unarguably the town's most scenic feature is the Cape Byron Lighthouse, built in 1901 above the cliffs of Australia's most easterly point. We decide to avoid atomisation by cellular phone for the afternoon and walk up to the Lighthouse in time to catch the sunset; on the way we pass densely-clustered coastal trees, populated in their lower regions by scurrying lizards, and occasionally opening up to reveal wide swathes of coastal waters fringed by sand and reflecting the late afternoon sun in dazzling shards and flashes. The wind picks up the further we get around the headland, with the sign which marks Australia's eastern tip marked visually on one side by waves pounding against rock and on the other by tourists gamely trying to take photos without having their phones blown over the edge or fighting losing battles to hold down their skirts. Face out to sea and behind you is an entire continent; in front, no significant land mass until you hit South America. This feeling of physical insignificance is something that you are unlikely to come across in the UK, surrounded as it is by larger bodies of land, or even on the continent with its smorgasbord of nation states and separate cultures within spitting distance of each other. If you want to feel dwarfed by the enormity of our planet, Cape Byron is a good place to do it.

In Australia this sense of being dwarfed by your environment can also be achieved by looking inwards, at the vast, sparsely inhabited centre. It is a feeling which, when your travels have been otherwise spent in heavily populated areas, can take some getting used to. Turn your back to the sea and a neat, well kept hippy town is laid out before you. Beyond this, the hinterlands and a deep green expanse of national parkland, moulded by ancient tectonic shifts. This greenery, while beautiful, is a visual siren song drawing the unwary traveller ever onwards; for beyond lies an even bigger expanse of scorched earth and snake venom. Myriad travellers, unprepared for the ferocity of heat and lack of sustenance, have perished in the outback. Urban Australia – mirroring a shipwrecked crew washed up on dry land, retching up saltwater bile and clinging to terra firma like a mother's teat – hugs the coastline with all its might and avoids looking too far inland, preferring myopia to the existential significance of all that looming space. It is akin to the sudden urge to jump when perched too close to the cliff edge; think too closely about all that space, hundreds of miles of sand and rock unconducive to the human condition, and any sense of time and space will begin to warp inexorably.

It is only the indigenous peoples of Australia who have truly assimilated in this vast red land, and the area around Byron gives the impression of immense size in a temporal as well as a spatial sense. Indigenous stories which have survived for millennia via word of mouth abound and one of the major Creation Myths of the Bundjalung Tribe, that of the Three Brothers, takes place amongst the local topography. The story varies slightly with different tellings, but the gist is that three brothers and their mother arrived on the shores of Northern New South Wales from foreign lands and the matriarch was somehow separated from her offspring (this is one of the few Dreamtime stories which sees ancestors arriving via boat from outside of the Australian continent). Believing this separation to be their doing she became enraged, whipping up a storm which caused the brothers to take shelter at nearby Ballina. Settling there and eventually deciding to explore the surrounding land, they helped shape the tenets which the Bundjalung people live by and also created the first Bora Ground, a sacred site in which the young males of the Eastern tribes would traditionally be initiated into manhood, at Lennox Head.

Somehow the patch of ground around the lighthouse, pretty much the highest in the area, is blocked off from the path of the wind; and so, by the time we sit down on a spot of grass amongst the many others who have had the same idea, the idyll has returned. The sun grows fatter and redder as it descends towards the horizon, picking up speed as it drops and casting hues of purples and yellows across the sky, artfully illuminating wisps of cloud in a spectacular display of solar resplendence. By the time we start back down twilight has truly descended and we pick our way through the undergrowth with care, mindful of snakes. A wrong turn sees tarmac crumble to soil crumble to sand as we enter an overgrown netherworld of thick vegetation, the pregnant moon lending an unearthly blue tone to what was verdant green only twenty minutes before as it drags the ocean inexorably up the shore. The soporific sound of waves lapping against sand increases the feeling of ethereal splendour which imbues the scene and, once I overcome my fear of stepping on irritable and venomous reptiles, our surroundings make the petty issues of day-to-day life seem far away. The original lighthouse keeper's cottages can be rented out as accommodation but, for those on a budget, watching the sun go down from the lighthouse is still the best activity that Byron has to offer; and an entirely free one at that.

The budget options on offer to us are hostel, campsite or free camping. The thought of spending our trip in backpacker hostels, trying to drink beers with and find common ground with 18 year olds, fills me with horror. Free camping is by far the cheapest way to see the country and there are various apps dedicated to finding the best spots to do so, but that option severely limits the locales available to you; so, by default, we find ourselves staying in campsites for most of the trip. The first spot in Byron proves to be one of the best, with a massive kitchen space and a wide range of travelling types ranging from 'Grey Nomads' – a growing Australian cultural movement which has seen retirees selling their homes and living out of caravans and trailers – to middle-aged hippies, to groups of travelling Europeans in their early 20s. The latter includes a group of young Italian couples who at first seem like fairly normal backpacker types; however it doesn't take anyone long to notice that, whenever one of the girls sits on the kitchen table, her partner immediately nestles his head into her crotch, closes his eyes and seemingly dozes off. As the kitchen table is where she sits through most of breakfast, this becomes a regular morning sight. Otherwise our fellow campers seem fairly well-adjusted, despite not being nearly as dedicated to finding good times late into the evening as we are.

Using Byron as a base, we venture out to the nearby villages of Bangalow and Nimbin. Bangalow consists of a handful of achingly twee streets full of carefully restored and heritage-listed buildings. They nearly all feature a small plaque detailing what their original purpose was, illustrated by faded black and white photographs from the turn of the century. It also, surprisingly, features an anomaly in the form of a small but gnarly concrete park with some of the most rugged pool coping I've skated this side of Oregon; the Australian equivalent of Saffron Walden, I suppose. I find out later that skaters from the surrounding area regularly make the trip for heavy evening sessions, but, not knowing this, we head through in the heat of the day and have the place to ourselves. Nimbin, further down the road, is the town which really gives the area its authentic hippy credentials. Host to the 1973 Aquarius Festival, the fourth instalment in an event which is seen by many as kickstarting the Australian hippy movement, the end of the festival saw a few psychedelically-enhanced attendees decide that this was the life for them. Hence, an ailing farming region was turned into a refuge for those seeking an alternative lifestyle and a legend was born.

We had planned to stop here for a couple of nights, but the general consensus was to give it an afternoon and no more. The story goes that for years the influx of cannabis into the town was controlled by one gang, with the police turning a blind eye due to the gang's refusal to allow anything stronger in (and, if random people I met at skateparks were to be believed, also due to a few kickbacks). This, in a country blighted by a meth epidemic, seems to me only sensible. However the draw of what was to all intents and purposes decriminalised weed meant that people started flocking in by the droves for the purpose of THC consumption. The government went into apoplexy over the thought that people might be growing, smoking and eating the buds from a plant. The police involved were stripped of their badges, the gang were arrested or dispersed and, of course, another group took over who weren't so picky about what substances they let in. What was once seen as a genuinely free place for smokers, hippies and those who wished to live off the land is now in danger of descending into squalor, and various people we spoke to told us not to leave valuables on display in the car, keep eyes on wallets and bags and other such cautionary tales. We were also told emphatically to avoid buying weed in the town, as police often wait on the outskirts to stop and search vehicles with out of state plates.

Suitably chastened when we reach Nimbin on a sweltering afternoon, we find that – as is so often the case with these kind of things – the reality nowhere near matches the hyperbole. Consisting of two main streets with a few winding side roads leading through rows of sprawling old houses, the town seems to be slightly frazzled but otherwise perfectly pleasant; despite a clear bent towards Camden Market style shops selling tourist memorabilia, crystals and bongs. And, to be honest, the levels of humidity which greeted us upon getting out of the car would leave me fairly frazzled. The quality of the town's backdrop, however, is undeniable – you can see why those first festival goers, slowly coming down and considering the return to reality at desk jobs in Sydney or farm life in any number of small hamlets dotted around the bush, decided not to leave. The town is surrounded on all sides by rising hills covered in a thick layer of greenery and the opportunities for tropical or mountainous walks seem endless. We get chatting to a scruffy older bloke with a tobacco stained beard, a former merchant seaman from Lewisham who had moved to Byron before the Trustafarians and the merciless tourism industry got too much for him. He'd moved to Nimbin with his wife and kids and hadn't looked back; "We've got six acres overlooking the forest... and I don't have a bit of money. It's fucking brilliant!" He's clearly a man who has found his niche in the world, though he does have certain misgivings about the town going the way of Byron and other such tourist sideshows.

He comes across us at Nimbin Skatepark, a place which I'd been excited to check out for awhile. He was proud of the park in that civic way which certain people have for their hometown's facilities, an abstract pride which does not necessarily have at its root an interest in that facility's primary purpose. He was right and the place doesn't disappoint – I'd say it stands as one of the best skateparks on the East Coast – but the air is so thick that, after twenty minutes of cruising down the snake run and into the bowl, I'm in genuine danger of ending up in hospital with serious dehydration. A day like today is good for one thing only, which is going to the pub, but being on driving duties means that I can only have a lemonade (and about five litres of water) whilst sitting on the veranda of the Nimbin Hotel. It's an incredibly scenic spot, but I'm now in Nimbin with no beer, no weed and no skateboarding; not an easy thing for me to get my head around. Hindsight is a horrible thing, but I have to say goodbye to Nimbin without really getting the experience I'd hoped for before attempting to drive down a mountain whilst suffering the beginnings of heatstroke.

Things have freshened up a little for our last day in Byron, which we spend stocking up on camping gear and perusing Howl and Moan records; a first for me, in that rather than being organised by genre and then alphabetically, the records are ordered strictly by the latter. Therefore, I get the experience for the first and probably last time in my life of leafing through a stack of vinyl to find UK hardcore punks Rot in Hell nestled next to Linda Ronstadt. That night we head to our first non-free pub gig of the trip, as General Levy is playing at the Beach Hotel for ten dollars – a ridiculously cheap entry price considering Australia's normally extortionate prices for visiting musicians. Maybe, despite a widespread obsession with Bob Marley – you'll hear him on a shop radio at least once a day in most of the more surf culture based towns down the coast, alongside entire T-shirt stalls dedicated to him – reggae-influenced music beyond the admittedly stellar output of the Tuff Gong hasn't quite penetrated popular culture Down Under. Whether or not this is the case, a crowd evenly split between backpackers and locals is definitely hyped for a dose of UK ragga.

The weather has gotten cooler still when we take our hangovers on the road to Ballina, home of our first 'Big Thing' of the trip. One of Australia's national quirks is the building of gaudy, oversized statues in various locations; raised for a variety of reasons which usually relate in some way to local history, agriculture or eminent local figures. Ballina, with its ocean location and long term fishing industry, boasts the Giant Prawn – a looming crustacean on the south side of town which, on weekends, sees seafood vendors set up stalls beneath its undercarriage to sell their wares. Midweek it is deserted, leaving us free to appreciate its majesty without distraction. Alongside a big shellfish, Ballina also boasts a bowl with a big-ish deep end – only nine foot, but a whippy nine foot which gives it the feel of an 80s vert ramp and keeps me on my toes. This is definitely not helped by the paint splashed by the council, presumably over graffiti, which throws in the occasional 'drifting wheel' sensation to spice things up. I get chatting to an old fella with the remnants of a joint poking out from the depths of an impressively smoke-stained grey beard, a local whose son skates but is currently out of town on a trip. He gives me a very welcome list of parks to hit all the way down the coast to Newcastle and shows me some clips on his phone of his son, of whom he is clearly (and rightfully so, after seeing the clips) proud. After a while more locals show up; a hippy dad who once lived in Brighton and skated The Level for a summer and his daughter both rip the bowl; a stocky, balding guy invites me to skate his miniramp after turning his leg at an unlikely angle and retiring to the injury bench; soon a whole group of skaters with ages ranging from early teens to mid 40s are creating clouds of smoke drifting along the beachfront while they drink and chat shit. This is why skateboarding can be the best and worst facilitator for travelling; the commonality is always there, but sometimes it can be too easy to stay within that comfort zone. That being said, after hitting a whole bunch of ghost town skateparks on the Gold Coast I'm more than happy for the company.

In Yamba, a picturesque town with a sweeping bay and the miniramp that dreams are made of, we go for a morning stroll on the breakwater and see a pod of dolphins frolicking in the water, two ospreys being bullied by a small but angry seagull and a manta ray jump vertically two feet out of the water before splashing back into the sparkling, turquoise sea. This is definitely a change of pace from London's foxes, rats and pigeons. We get chatting to a middle-aged couple from Newcastle (the Australian one) who tell us about their horror at house prices in London and Paris when they traveled through Europe, "... so we booked a cheaper place 20 minutes outside the centre (of Paris), got on the train, then as we got towards the place realised it was just full of black people... it was alright though." Australia might not be the shockingly outright racist society of Paul Theroux's *The Happy Isles of Oceania* anymore, but the casual racism of the older (and sometimes younger) generation is so relentless it can reach farcical proportions. Australians can be almost defensive in their backhanded mentions of race when in conversation; "and there were a lot of black people there"; "and the bloke was Asian, so..."; it seems to cling desperately to a notion of Aussie reactionary opinions which would make Jeremy Clarkson blush. If Jim Davidson was raised here, he would have a successful career in politics by now.

CHAPTER FOUR

Discovering Macquarie

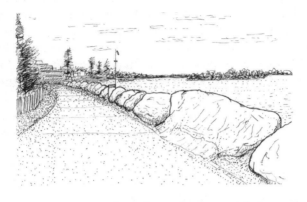

The small coastal town of Coffs Harbour, nestled on the Eastern coast of New South Wales around the halfway mark between Brisbane and Newcastle, plays host to a cultural powerhouse in the form of Australia's only dedicated cartoon gallery The Bunker. When we pass through Coffs on our way down the coast this Australian institution, housed in an underground WWII bunker, is hosting an exhibition focusing on political cartoons featured in newspapers over the course of 2017. The structure, with all its inherent connotations of international dischord, political intrigue and impending fiery doom, is nothing if not relevant to the political climate of these first few vicious years of the 21st century. It provides a fitting home to a selection of illustrations offering an insight into the tangled web of Australian politics, a subject which only seems to get more convoluted upon closer inspection (they've had five prime ministers since 2010). It also acts as a timely reminder as to just how well Pauline Hanson can tread a tightrope between 'evil' and 'insane' and still somehow strike a chord with voters. Australia is, of course, the country where a young Rupert Murdoch began constructing his empire, and Hanson is yet another political manifestation of the dark side of the Antipodean psyche. Despite its immense geographical size, in Australia it is all too common to encounter an islander's isolationist mentality –

something grimly ironic considering the indigenous displacement and exploitation upon which the country's urban sprawl is built. Various conversations overheard already by this point of the trip have highlighted the all-pervasive influence of the Murdoch press on public opinion, something all too familiar when you've grown up in the UK. Now at The Bunker these bitingly accurate works of satire give me a much clearer idea of just how pernicious a hold racism and right wing ideologies have in mainstream politics and the public sphere. The work of First Dog On The Moon in particular deals with some of the issues currently facing the nation with a hearteningly bleak sense of humour, and I highly recommend looking it up online and treating yourself to a despairing chuckle or two. A walk across the breakwater to Muttonbird Island Nature Reserve highlights the great work done by conservationists in the area, but by now I'm truly terrified for the future of the human race and it'll take more than a few safe seabird eggs to convince me otherwise.

Driving inland to Bellingen for a break from coastal towns – the constant squawk of gulls and taste of salt in the air and the strange uniformity of seaside resort destinations – we find a village nestled deep in a valley between sea and mountains which boasts one of the oddest but most fun parks we've found on the road so far. Bellingen Skatepark is an abstract, jumbled mess, new park standing shoulder to shoulder with old in avant garde perplexity in which the user can salvage a surprising amount of fun from inherent dysfunction. The river flowing next to it, one which in appearance could well run through a bucolic English village, is apparently the spot of choice to witness a spectacular early evening migration of bats from sea to mountain which is promised by the *Lonely Planet*. This never materialises during our stay, but the spectacular sunsets which act as a backdrop to my less than spectacular frontside grinds more than make up for any lack of flying mammal. "The town also boasts a skate scene to go with the park, not always a given in a country where inhabited areas are so spread out. Endorphins already high from the adrenalin and from the shared enjoyment of a session with others, the exchange of experiences and shared cultural knowledge which lubricates this kind of travel so well, we head for a nearby pub. An unwillingness to finish the skate session too early means that we miss last orders on food by an hour, but this is no problem for the barman at the Federal Hotel; who manages to find some leftover lasagne and charges us next to nothing for it, apologising all the while for the lack of garnish to go alongside it. Cheers to him for cementing Bellingen as one of the best stopping points of our journey."

Heading back to the coast to continue south, a car rally taking place in Nambucca Heads sees us detour to Macksville in search of accommodation. This turns out to be a small, seedy but friendly town where we luck out and end up staying above a pub with a balcony opening onto the broad Nambucca River. The Star Hotel has an impressive, Wild West saloon-channeling facade, a large bar and a mixture of locals and rally enthusiasts all necking booze with the same intent of getting rat arsed and dancing to the blues/funk covers band on stage. Not only are the vibes good, but we hit big in the evening's meat raffle (a staple of Australian pub life) and win enough cuts of meat to feed a family of five for a week.

Less luck is had with the local skatepark; the internet offers up photos of what looks to be the spitting image of Slade's Farm in Bournemouth, but it turns out that the bowl has been demolished and replaced with a passable but fairly bog standard modern park layout. A five foot miniramp would normally put me in a good mood but the knowledge of what used to sit here sours the place for me; it reeks of the kind of attitude that would blithely describe Clapham Common skatepark as better than Stockwell and not even blink, the kind of attitude that can only lead to enforced surgery removing some of skateboarding's most alluring warts. It's Cliff Richard rather than Motorhead, *Avatar* rather than *Repo Man*. Not that I'm completely rubbishing the construction of well built, basic skateparks; that would be more than a little hypocritical, given how much of my life I've spent in parks both good and bad over the years. It's easy to see the Gramscian train of thought involved in a council's decision to build a skatepark – give the kids a skatepark and they won't be out skating on the streets, interacting with their environment and subverting norms of how public space is viewed. Consent is manufactured, hegemonic control is maintained. But the skatepark, when moulded by the hands of a good local scene, takes on a life of its own. It becomes the warm up spot before we hit the streets harder than ever, it becomes its own social bubble where younger skaters are schooled in civil disobedience by older ones, it is policed better by its users than by the police themselves. Like the Geto Boys in '91, we can't be stopped – what at first seems like hegemonic control is entirely subverted by the intended user group and these skateparks in an ideal world funnel their users into the same public spaces they were designed to keep us out of. In a town like Macksville however, where I see little evidence of a skate scene, what once would have been a draw for hunters of obscure concrete relics like yours truly, a uniquely gnarly park with a unique skate scene to match, becomes just another dot on the map.

Port Macquarie is similarly modern, but my lack of expectations otherwise means that it doesn't incur any sense of righteous ire within me. Unfortunately, and presumably due to the locale of the build right next to the town's major caravan park, it is overrun with kids for the entirety of the Saturday and Sunday we spend there. It is only on the Monday when a full-on session is possible and even then, by 10:30am, I'm passive aggressively muttering about the place being 'more of a fucking creche than a skatepark' within hearing range of clueless parents. Pushing down the boardwalk is a much less stressful experience, with a scenic stretch of water enhanced by the breakwater rocks bursting with colour from murals painted by local residents.

These range from commemorations of deceased loved ones to celebrations of regular holiday visits, with one even boasting a scoop of DIY concrete turning it into a vaguely skateable quarterpipe; something which the crashing ocean waves just beyond the lip dissuade me from testing out. It is the perfect sunset locale in which to crack a beer, watch pods of dolphins scythe through the water and chat shit with the local fishermen, and we take full advantage of that.

On our last morning in the town, the car left at a mechanic's with various problems incomprehensible to the likes of me, we head to the Glasshouse – a large modern building which acts as Port Macquarie's cultural hub in its curation of art exhibitions, gigs and theatrical shows. Upon entering its imposingly modern glass and steel facade, the visitor is greeted by a row of glass cabinets detailing the history of Port; from the indigenous Birpai community's honey gathering techniques, through to European invasion and convict settlement. The timber industry quickly took hold in the area once the settlers came, forever changing the landscape that the local Birpai residents subsisted on. The township settlement, meanwhile, was overseen in no small part by Scottish born Lachlan Macquarie; the governor for whom the port, and seemingly half of New South Wales, is named. Lachlan was seen as a soft touch and reformist by many at the time, for statements like this one:

"In no case must more than fifty lashes be inflicted on any man whatever his crime may be. Instead solitary confinement on bread and water, for a reasonable time, or extra hard labour for minor offences should be given."

Compared to his stance on indigenous people, this was positively philanthropic. In Jason Wing's exhibition 'The Presence of Absence', a quote from Macquarie takes centre stage which proclaims:

"All aborigines from Sydney onwards are to be made prisoners of war and if they resist they are to be shot and their bodies hung from the trees in the most conspicuous places near where they fall, so as to strike terror into the hearts of the surviving natives."

If the Nobel Peace Prize had been around at this time, Lachlan's chances of winning would have been slim. The exhibition also deals with modern, more subtle methods of submerging indigenous cultures and does not ignore white Australia's still sketchy relationship with racial issues:

"Fundamentally nothing has changed in 248 years. The violent and racist legacy left by Captain James Cook and his fellow colonisers is enmeshed in the foundation of contemporary Australian society."

A powerful and unsettling body of work which we had entirely to ourselves on a sunny Tuesday afternoon, it offered a compelling insight into Australia's hidden history which is only now starting to be delved further into by the rest of the world; one made all the more powerful by its location in the centre of a town named for a governor who had no qualms in ordering the execution of Aboriginal people who would defy him.

CHAPTER FIVE

Bad elements and aggressive achievements

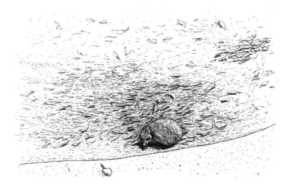

"I'm sure you can tell who the bad elements are – they were selling the pot, the reefer, whatever you call it in the UK... and worse." Heavy set, crew cut, an ex-police officer with poor dental hygiene and a map of broken capillaries tracing their way across his bovine face, he is a character straight from the police convention in *Fear and Loathing* that even Ralph Steadman would have balked at drawing in his full glory; and he has decided that, as the only other adult in the skatepark, I am going to be his friend.

Back in Port Macquarie, on our way to pick up the car from the garage, we wander past a sign inviting people into an artificial plant shop which boldly states in large lettering

"BE HUMBLE WITH CONFIDENCE AND AGGRESSIVE IN ACHIEVEMENTS!"

As a motto for artificial plants, this must be up there with the most bizarrely intense, but if anyone has something more incongruous then please let me know – 'Doris' Plant Emporium: Death Before Dishonour', or 'Ethel's Artfully Artificial Flowers: If It Bleeds, We Can Kill It' – that sort of thing. After a morning coming to terms with white Australia's bloody history, this kind of eccentricity comes as a welcome mood lightener.

Heading on down the road, we take heed of some much-parroted advice and detour to the small town of Forster. Numerous chance acquaintances up and down the coast have waxed lyrical over its aesthetic charms, but after a couple of weeks of non-stop coastal meandering – endless rows of Op Shops, cafes overflowing with pensioners, off-season dead nightlife, sea air, sand burn and sand flies – I am reaching beach resort town overload. Waking up to find a steady drizzle taking hold does nothing to alleviate this, but we attempt to salvage the day by negotiating the only marked bush walk which starts from the campsite anyway. This turns out to be a big mistake – we are immediately swarmed by clouds of the largest and most persistent mosquitoes we've seen in the country, with our pitiful layer of Aerogard seeming only to infuriate or arouse them. We find ourselves running back to our site and the safety of the enclosed camp kitchen, where the only thing for the day is to put a slab of beer in the fridge and start boozing until the weather clears. As we are staying a good few kilometres down the motorway from town, and the rain doesn't stop until sunset (which to be fair, is incredible), once it does clear then there's nothing to do but keep boozing. Sitting drunk on the toilet that night, blearily watching a broken-legged cockroach gimp its way unsteadily back and forth across the cubicle floor, I realise that some time in a city is probably needed.

This leads us to Newcastle, Charlestown Skatepark, and my new pal. Charlestown has been on the lips of someone at nearly every skatepark I've visited down the coast and doesn't disappoint, with a well laid out flow bowl and large kidney bowl offering up a wide array of lines. Despite a heavy teenage presence I still get the park nearly to myself, with the locals being more interested in lurking, smoking cigs and nearly getting in fights with other groups of testosterone-fuelled adolescents than using the variety of scooters and skateboards they have to hand. Despite their Lord of the Flies-influenced approach to each other, towards me they offer either complete indifference or wary politeness, so I'm free to skate to my hearts content until I'm approached by this alumni of Australia's fine keepers of the peace. He lowers his voice to a stage whisper as he tells me of the recently installed CCTV and its success in curbing the previously mentioned herbal activities before denouncing the teenage girls stopping in from the nearby mall as 'skanks', a term he applies to a wide array of women who crop up over the course of his singularly monotonous conversation (the males are merely 'bad elements' or occasionally 'gronks'). Alyce shows up in time for him to tell us that "I skated when I was a kid, but I was nearly as bad as some of the girls", and when we protest he shoots us a triumphant look; "But these girls who skate good – are they ladies ?" I mentally curse him with gout, syphilis, dengue fever, rabies, a plague of sandflies burrowing through his bellend and exploding in glorious, agonising freedom from his pisshole, before we make our escape.

Heading to a gig at The Lass O'Gowrie, a reassuringly spit-and-sawdust bar, we walk in to find a band called Medheads opening their set with a cover of Devo's 'Gut Feeling'. This goes some way to restoring our equilibrium, but the thought still nags at the back of my mind; what if this caricature of institutionalised cop stupidity is not in the minority? It is a terrifying thought, one which causes me to mentally let fly a further flurry of misfortune upon his person, a thought which I hope won't be borne out by the rest of my trip. A brilliantly fast, fun and irreverent set from Medheads as well as feminist punks Glitoris' theatrically heavy headlining set helps to allay these fears; I can only hope that his young son, who bears the brunt of his poisonous drivel, dedicates the rest of his formative years to fully-fledged creative, spontaneous, fuck you rebellion against this entrenched reactionary pig bullshit.

Charlestown is on the gnarlier end of the scale as bowls go, as is Bar Beach, but Newcastle has its share of more relaxed parks as well; Swansea Skatepark acts as a shining beacon for what a low altitude skatepark should be, while Elermore Vale and Islington Skateparks make up for in crust what they lack in depth; a very different kettle of gnar to Charlestown or Bar Beach, clearly created by cowboy builders and both with a concrete noping lip, I have both these kinked dishes to myself and am free to give in to my wildest early grab desires. Islington even chucks some karma points my way, when we arrive to find a possum trapped in the bowl and bodge together a tree branch ladder to aid its escape before a happy couple of hours spent rolling around in concrete dust and marsupial shit. The city itself, despite being the second largest in New South Wales, feels small; with only a short drive finding you deep in the hills and valleys of the Hunter Valley, home of world-renowned wineries and wild tracts of natural wonder which sit under a haze of smoke from distant bushfires during our stay. A raging wind spreads embers far and wide somewhere else in the valley but – beyond making for a hairy ride as we are buffeted from either side at the point where the Pacific Highway crosses the Hunter River – somehow does not impact on our journey into or out of the city.

Coming out of the suburbs we find a city centre which feels more spacious than Brisbane, Sydney or Melbourne, peppered with remnants of its industrial past and opening onto an expanse of beach which, with its painted railings, ice cream stands and domed rotundas, evokes the fading seaside resorts which pepper the shores of Britain. Only a burnt out pier or two is needed to complete the picture. Newcastle's industrial look comes from its position as a former centre of Australia's steel industry, an industry explained in detail by a short but entertaining audiovisual show in the Newcastle Museum. This sees a full sized ladle travel on beams across the roof in a simulated steelworks environment – a noisy, chaotic experience with smoke and flashing lights which has clearly terrified three children who have been brought to enjoy the experience. Their harried-looking parents are attempting to explain that this is fun they are having, look at how fun it all is; but their drooping postures attest to the slow realisation that the centrepoint of their day trip to the city is going down like the proverbial lead (steel?) balloon. Away from fake furnaces and the piercing squeals of childhood terror, the museum is also informative when it comes to the entertainment available to 18th century Novocastrians and features one of the best pieces of museum literature I have had the pleasure of reading:

"The people of Hamilton had no need to travel to town for entertainment as on this corner where the Kent Hotel now stands, Monty Beecroft ran Massey's Dog Circus, a steam-driven Merry-Go-Round, a joyride called the Razzle Dazzle and a 'Blondin' tightrope walking show. Mr Massey would often parade his performers down Beaumont Street to perform an open air dog circus on the future site of the Roxy Theatre. One of Massey's dogs, a fox terrier, assumed moderate fame as it would eat meat six days a week but would only eat fish on Fridays."

If only the activities on offer in Newcastle today could match these heady pleasures; but, even as it stands, Australia's steel city is a pleasant surprise. We arrived with few expectations but it seems that, under the baleful gaze and frothing rhetoric of the city's establishment, a younger generation has created a thriving cultural milieu.

CHAPTER SIX

Dreamtime myths and cosmic prolapses

The heavens repeatedly open on us in the Central Coast, meaning I squeeze in only one brief skate at the brand new Bateau Bay Skatepark and witness what can only be, in a just world, the future of skatepark construction. Apart from this revelation in skatepark design, two days of complete downpour means that judgements on this stretch of Australia's East Coast will have to wait until another visit.

We reach Sydney just before alt rock legends The Breeders hit no less venerable a venue than the Sydney Opera House, and our first Friday night in Sydney finds me cursing both the exorbitant prices and my own skinflint ways as I resist the urge to down my ten dollar stubby with joy at the opening chords of 'Divine Hammer'. The gig is nothing short of brilliant, but such a band playing at the Opera House doesn't necessarily give me hope for the city's music scene. Sydney sprawls in elegant pretension around its iconic harbour, at first glance, a place so bloated by its own good looks that it barely feels the need to advance anything which doesn't fit into the parameters of upper middle class snobbery. Underneath this pomposity seethes a maelstrom of discontent, street fights and shooting galleries and the ravaging wind of crystal meth, more damaging than an army of cane toads. Repeated attempts to stamp out all that is good and dangerous about youth culture haven't been entirely successful – music and art can't help but thrive in such adverse conditions – but cultural stagnation must surely lie somewhere along the path that Sydney's politicians and upper classes are heading down and they would do well to heed the anger flowing through the streets.

Misgivings aside, Sydney is a welcome return to noisy, dirty, sprawling city life. A lot can be forgiven of a place where you can bask in the heat on the waterfront of the Botanical Gardens, watching fragments of the sun's reflection ping from the Opera House and letting the ocean breeze whistle mournfully across the top of your beer bottle. Its innumerable bays and inlets offer boundless opportunities for exploration, with hills that can send you plunging from tourist hell to idyllic ocean cove with disorienting suddenness. The city's many nooks and crannies have also been a palate for the good, the bad and the ugly of skatepark construction companies for decades. It is our last stop of any length before we reach Melbourne and, with not much idea of what lay between skate-wise (besides a few legendary Canberra gems), a nonstop rotation of street beers and gnarly transitions with the crew showing me around the city's many skateparks is not taken for granted. While its music and arts scenes may be suffering, Sydney's skate scene seems as strong as ever.

My pilgrimage starts with Manly Vale. This is one of Sydney's lesser skated gems, which clearly doesn't get much love as pre-skate necessities include shifting an abandoned mountain bike and sweeping large quantities of broken glass into the corner I think I'm least likely to slam in. With this community service complete I get stuck into possibly the best kidney pool in the world, which I make a point of visiting every time I find myself nearby and which I dream of one day having recreated in my garden. Towards the end of a quiet, humid day which sees me with the place mostly to myself, I'm joined by some curious kids on scooters. One of them asks me if he should try and drop in to the shallow end and without thinking I tell him it's probably too steep; in fact it would be easier in the deep end, as there's more transition to work with. He takes my word as gospel and hurls himself into the deep with the enthusiasm of a 1930s banker exiting a skyscraper, hitting the flat with the kind of noise that would bring any concerned parent running – but skateparks work just as well as playgrounds when it comes to leaving small children to their own devices, right? He climbs out by himself, but getting to the bus stop proves more of a challenge with his ankle swelling up like a balloon. Feeling slightly responsible, I let him use my board as a crutch before heading back to finish my six pack and squeeze in a few more slash grinds before my legs give out and I find a similar fate.

The week soon becomes an endurance test for my legs, from the uniquely gnarly old concrete of Galston to the brand new build at Sydenham and all points in between. Sunday brings with it fresher weather, a strong breeze and a session at the vert ramp dreams are made of with a crew of local rippers. A ten footer originating in the murky depths of the 80s, recently re-skimmed for maximum speed, the afternoon's fun is only slightly hampered by the wind. Intermittent gusts rage across the adjacent field, often just as wheels reach the lip of the ramp, turning even the humble 5050 into a white knuckle ride threatening to send the rider hurtling headlong into the abyss.

The week of non stop skatepark charging takes its toll and, when we head for Katoomba in the depths of the Blue Mountains the next day, I opt to leave my board in Sydney and concentrate on the area's natural bounty. An indica-enhanced sunset at Echo Point that first night frames vertiginous green freefall into the depths of nature's disorder, darker shades slowly overwhelm the light as the sun is swallowed by the horizon and blots out our first glimpse of the area's ancient grandeur which even now is imprinted on my eyelids. The next morning we trek to Leura Falls and wind our way back towards the Three Sisters, descending and ascending hundreds of stairs and passing waterfalls, lookouts and rock formations moulded by millions of years of weather with increasing wonderment. The Three Sisters dominate the landscape, both literally and figuratively. One of the most enduring stories repeated by the Blue Mountains Tourist Board tells of the three beautiful daughters - Meehni, Wimlah and Gunnedoo - of a local witch doctor. Told not to enter the Jamison Valley, inhabited as it was by one of the fearsome Bunyips which haunt Aboriginal legend, their curiosity got the better of them and whilst peeking over the cliff edge they managed to dislodge some rocks and wake the beast. Sensing an unexpected but easy breakfast, the Bunyip quickly began ascending the cliff face when their quick thinking father used his magic stick to turn the sisters into three pillars of rock. With the enraged and possibly now very hungry creature's attentions now directed towards him, the good doctor turned himself into a lyrebird to escape into the bush but during this escape lost his stick and was left unable to transform himself or his daughters back into human form. He can still be seen to this day, scratching through the bush in search for the instrument to bring about this transformation.

The catch is, the tale was not as integral to local Indigenous history as it at first seems; according to various sources it was woven by a white schoolgirl by the serendipitous name of Patricia Stone. Catching on fast, the story went beyond a few naive tourists to become part of the local tourism department's literature while the local Gundungurra tribe pissed themselves laughing at the gullible visitors, keeping the real story to themselves.

A couple of hours into our walk, we hear a crashing through the undergrowth and a fully grown lyrebird with resplendent tailfeathers scurries across the path ten feet in front of us. Fact and fiction blur as we wonder if this is the good doctor of legend, whether such a legend even existed at all, but a glimpse of such an iconic and reclusive creature is a cause for celebration either way. It's presence is still resonating when, further down the path, we pass two German girls who warn us that the views ahead are nothing to write home about.I don't want to cast aspersions on either their eyesight or their ability to appreciate their surroundings, but following on from this caution we reach Bridal Veil Lookout and find the enormity of the Blue Mountains spread out before us in all its glory. Fecund hills and valleys dappled by the chiaroscuro of cloud and sun lie in seeming slumber, a scene straight out of a Hollywood film introducing the audience to a lost world; its prehistoric cast aided by the primordial shriek of raucous cockatoos, by now a familiar sound on our travels. They may look pretty, but if you ever wonder what a dinosaur slaughterhouse would sound like then cockatoos are probably as close an answer as you are going to get.

Back in the city the concrete pilgrimage continues, covering wide swathes of Sydney's urban sprawl in a mission to hit as many skateparks as possible from Thursday to Sunday. At Maroubra Skatepark, home to one of Sydney's biggest surf enclaves, I not only manage to convince a horde of children to remove themselves from the bowl but also to act as assistants when my board went AWOL and retrieve it from far flung corners of the park. I toy with the idea of sending them en masse onto the beaches – rifling swimmer's clothes for cash, minesweeping drinks from pricey beachfront bars and returning with their ill-gotten gains – but in this heat the thought of becoming a crime overlord is much too tiring and I stick to the bowl. Our time in Sydney finishes with a reunion with the legendary Five Dock for the first time in a couple of years, but the previous few days still prey on my legs and I don't have much for such a demanding bowl. After a few half-arsed runs I retire to the skinning-up bench, where we are joined by a rake-thin meth casualty who has moved on from the rollerblades he started the session on and is now flailing around the park on a haggard old board. Far too young for the thousand-yard stare he sports, the muscles of his jaw twitching spasmodically like a knackered sewing machine, he makes only a token effort at small talk. "Hard work this bowl, isn't it? .. Even harder with a punctured lung, which i'm recovering from. I was in a car accident, it was only luck that my kid wasn't in the car with me." He then dives into his tale of misery, hereditary organ issues, car accidents and collapsed lungs ("because of painkillers" later changed to "smoking too many bongs"). A scrawny, bug-eyed, dilated pupil, ceaselessly twitching harbinger of the green-out, oozing bad vibes as if from open sores on his skin, he instigates a quick exit for the rest of us.

We leave Sydney for Canberra (home of The Big Owl and The Big Mushroom) as clouds build in the distance and, before we are more than a quarter of the way there, Armagideon has descended and the storm has crossed our path with the vehemence of a red-ragged bull – torrential rain, pebble-sized hailstones, forks of electricity striking nearby paddocks in a cosmic prolapse of religious proportions. It is a terrifying, exhilarating drive which at one point sees the majority of road users pulled up on the hard shoulder until visibility improves and the streams criss-crossing the highway begin to thin to a trickle. Unsurprisingly this sees the next day written off, while also opening up the justification for an extra day in the nation's capital with the main road through to Melbourne flooded. I make the most of it by heading straight to the legendary Belconnen, whose pit of a bowl is instantly recognisable from a plethora of skate videos. The bowl is everything I'd hoped for but the newer, larger section disappoints, so after an hour of solo carving I decide to skate the eight kilometres to The Yard Skatepark, glimpsed through intermittent squalls while exploring the city centre the previous day. This turns out to be a bigger undertaking than Google Maps tells me, taking in motorways, gravel roads through nature reserves and rural hillbombs, all leading to one of the surprise hits of the Australian Capital Territory; a tightly packed park which flows surprisingly well, despite the all-encompassing broken glass which my best efforts could only dint. One day someone will write a thesis on the Australian psyche and its propensity to see skateparks as receptacles for glass recycling; for now, society only has my futile rants on paper to warn of this national pastime.

Canberra itself is much maligned as a cultural cul-de-sac, only taking on the role of capital because the respective governments of Sydney and Melbourne couldn't figure out which one of them should be given the honour. Undoubtedly it doesn't have the aesthetic charms of Sydney's Victorian grandeur, or Melbourne's scuzzy industrial canvas for street artists – indeed, its endless blocks of flats with their built in gyms, restaurants and pools bring to mind nothing so much as JG Ballard's nightmarish future vision in *High Rise* – but, ignoring its obvious architectural shortcomings, it offers up an array of skateparks, cheap bars, good food and legal cannabis in abundance. The city's galleries feature a number of well curated exhibitions, including one in which artist Trevor Dickinson has created a visual ode to Canberra's distinctive bus shelters. This lauding of a brutalist architectural oddity is peculiarly skater-like in its obsessiveness and opposition to popular architectural opinion. It might be expressed via a different medium, but I bet Dickinson would have backed the LLSB campaign if he lived in London rather than Canberra.

Canberra is one of the world's few entirely planned cities, designed by Walter Burley Griffin and Marion Mahony Griffin around various geometric motifs and with natural vegetation planned as a defining feature. As such, when seen from above it resembles nothing so much as a gigantic formal garden, or perhaps a series of crop circles put down by particularly unimaginative aliens. It's name is thought to have been derived from a word used by the Ngunnawal, the local indigenous tribe, which means either 'meeting place' or 'woman's breasts' depending on who you speak to. The 'woman's breasts' theory definitely flies, at least if you squint your eyes whilst looking in the right direction; two mountains, Mount Ainslie and the Black Mountain, are close enough to each other to connect the name to a topographical feature. The irony of a completely pre-planned city being labelled with a word which relates so specifically to natural landmarks, and is so indicative of the Aboriginal connection to the land, is one that I can imagine is not lost on the descendents of the Ngunnawal. Nature cultivated and bent to the will of man in neat, orderly rows and circles, it hardly inspires the same primal emotion as some of the places we've passed through on the way down the coast.

Over three days exploring the city, we repeatedly pass the sprawl of Old Parliament House gleaming white against the landscaping. On its carefully manicured lawn, a few scattered tents and signs sway gently in the wind. Parliament House, the centre of Australia's policy-making establishment, may now be housed further up the hill, but this innocuous array of fabric and canvas is a reminder of an event writ large in the fight for Aboriginal justice, and of all the wrongs perpetrated through successive government policies before and since. In the early days of 1972, then Prime Minister William McMahon made a statement which continued White Australia's denial of Aboriginal land rights. Coming as it did at a time when the American Civil Rights movement was in full swing and their Black Panther party had helped to inspire the recent formation of the Australian Black Panthers, protests took place immediately and culminated in the staking out of tents in front of Parliament House – the Aboriginal Embassy. The tents popped up in ever greater numbers over the ensuing months and it wasn't until July that the government was able to pass new ordinance making it illegal to camp outside parliament. Two violent police raids to clear the tents brought about the physical end of the original Embassy, but tents continued to spring up and come down over the ensuing years and the long lasting impact of the protest is still felt today.

Once the flood waters have receded enough to make progress, we head towards Albury via the expertly named 'Dog On a Tuckerbox' – not a Big Thing, but rather a normal-sized statue of a dog on a lunchbox which, when it was unveiled in 1932, proved to be a big tourist draw and even inspired a song (Jack O'Hagan's 1937 'Where the Dog Sits on the Tuckerbox (Five Miles From Gundagai)'). Clearly rural Australia in the 1930s was punching above its weight when it came to contributions to popular culture. Luckily – to help placate the righteous ire of modern travellers spoilt by technological advancement, a rise in disposable income levels and the subsequent increase in travel as leisure – the authorities have installed a Big Koala around the corner.

Our taste for comically large statues thus sated, we continued on our drive to Melbourne through an arid landscape of near Wild West proportions; sun baked hills and gullies, dead, twisted tree branches, a hillbilly's smorgasbord of roadkill and cattle skulls so artfully placed that they may well have been dropped off as part of an initiative by the Hume Highway tourism board. Sun-blasted two-street towns spring up from the soil like concrete mushrooms, peopled by weatherbeaten farmers or sleekly well-fed retirees and wine growers depending on the area's affluence. The eccentricity of these outposts vary from amusing to offensive, as do the skateparks found within them; Holbrook (ankle-breaking six inch high handrail, submarine museum, large submarine replica in town centre, decidedly inland), Albury (kinked metal vert ramp, bizarre bowled out flatbanks, ankle-breaking six inch high handrail part two), Glenrowan (Big Ned Kelly, unfortunately we turn up too late in the day for the 'Ned Kelly Animatronic Experience') and Benalla – home to a surprisingly modern skatepark, if geared more towards BMXers than skateboarders. Sitting alongside an art gallery from which you could pay to be guided through the kind of street art tours you'd find in Shoreditch or Manhattan, it was clear that we were again approaching urban Australia.

Before Benalla, however, we stop in Beechworth on the recommendation of an Albury cafe owner who waxes lyrical about the town's quaintness, its historical importance and its traditional sweet shop. This sweet shop turns out to follow tradition far further than is acceptable, giving over one wall to a golliwog display that would make a UKIP voting West Country redneck in the most inbred Cornish town blush. The ruined hospital, restored historic houses and gaol are all pleasant, but when we get low on gas and find that the only service station in town has run out – and most of the restaurants are already closed – then we're faced with the unpleasant prospect of spending the night here with only racist sweets for sustenance. Luckily the bar staff at a nearby brewery direct us to an even smaller town which, without the tourist draw of offensive children's dolls, has managed to maintain its supply of petrol despite being cut off by flooding for the last four days. We fill the tank and drive on into the steadily deepening indigo of a warm summer evening, flanked by the rolling hills of rural Victoria and only mildly apprehensive that, whatever the next stop brings us, it will be home for the foreseeable future.

CHAPTER SEVEN

Minimalist techno living specialty coffee

Not long after our arrival in Melbourne, hunting the web for cheap or free furnishings for our room, I stumble across a huge box of books being gifted by someone a couple of suburbs up the road from our new home in Coburg. Once I've weeded out the crap (*How to Become a Bitcoin Millionaire*, *Convert Likes into Cash*, etc.), I'm left with a selection of modern classics ranging from Miller to Joyce to a pretty extensive selection of Kurt Vonnegut.

Getting stuck into one of these latter reads, the meta-masterpiece *Breakfast of Champions*, sees me through a couple of 40 degree days where leaving the house is almost an impossibility and I need a break from constantly scouring the shop windows for help wanted signs. I am struck by the passage in which the character Kilgore Trout looks from a car window "...out at the countryside, which was smeared by high velocity." All the way down to Melbourne our surroundings have been near-constantly smeared by high velocity, but I have no idea if sharp focus will assist in my writing or if the smear, like an impressionistic muse, is needed to maintain literary momentum. Can a travel book continue once the destination implied from the beginning has been reached? Does the word 'travel' naturally imply a destination, rather than the kind of continuous movement which can still take place within the confines of whatever that destination might be?

These thoughts dominate for the first few weeks in Melbourne, tramping the streets or sitting in front of a laptop desperately applying for any and all jobs in order to replete our decimated savings. A nagging doubt in the back of my head starts wondering if my plans have resulted in nothing more than me detailing my failed attempts at getting employment with a supermarket chain and then hurling them into the internet void. Bukowski already had the last word in the endless drudgery of job hunting and menial roles and, besides, I don't like booze enough to want it for breakfast.

To pass the time, and to keep myself from losing my mental bearings completely to cyberspace, in between scouring job sites and handing out CV's I walk and skate the streets from Coburg to the CBD and from the Eastern to Western suburbs. I drink in the city's aesthetics, its anomalies and accidents, its street scenes which at their best confound the viewer as if they were some avant garde piece of performance art; two commuters running for two trams on an unavoidable collision course; a topless, sinewy biker sitting on a bench, repeatedly spitting clots of blood onto the floor and cackling at what his lungs produce; an old casualty of the streets stumbling onto the tram, with arms full of various half drunk soft drink containers, losing his footing and spilling sugary liquid all over me. The extensive street art which adorns the buildings, the ethnic diversity of the restaurants, the hysterical, posturing anarchist flyers, the pretentious, overpriced bars and cafes – one job board offering states that a role has opened at a 'Minimalist techno living specialty coffee and bagel' joint – all become familiar sights. Melbourne's skyline, an otherwise unassuming silhouette, can from miles around be glimpsed through the gaps in suburbia's whitened teeth like some gargantuan voyeur of its own corpulent extremities. Its constant presence distorts any sense of distance, making the city feel much smaller than it is in reality. When the temperature soars the winds from the Southern Ocean do nothing to alleviate discomfort, battering the senses mercilessly with the sensation of standing in front of a recently opened oven door. Occasionally the heat whips itself into a thunderstorm, sending walkers scurrying to the nearest bar where the old drinkers with their blocked-drain laughter pass the time of day and their burst capillaries create paths, highways, maps of towns long passed into the ruin of nights previous. The skint merely take refuge under the nearest awning, forlorn with boredom until the weather lets up or impending ennui impels them into the deluge.

Large urban areas, concentrations of thousands and millions of people, personalities and dreams, cannot fail to buzz with cosmic forces beyond the ken of the keenest anthropologist. That buzz will be myriad different things to myriad different people but it will undoubtedly be there, humming just below the surface of consciousness like the live rail on a train track – the city's unique personality. On the first night we spend in Melbourne, sipping on a beer not long after the clock strikes midnight, I hear a board rattling past on the street below and take it as a good omen. I have Coburg's kidney pool all to myself for a number of sessions and take full advantage, becoming intimately aware of its kinks and quirks, the leak which springs from halfway up the transition opposite the hip, the almost gravel flat bottom. As a postscript to our possum rescue in Newcastle, one day I find a rat trapped in the bowl. Borrowing a hessian sack from a gardener in a nearby house, the rat is soon caught and set free to shred spots more within its means. I spend a couple of evenings reading Anthony Bourdain's culinary travel book *A Cook's Tour* and contemplating the motives of those who attempt to share their travel experiences with others. Mine may not reach the same spikes of adrenaline as those of Bourdain – no homemade whiskey with the Khmer Rouge or still-beating snake's heart entrees – but then this is one of those multiple and unexpected mental side benefits of skateboarding. The human need for excitement, instead of spiking intermittently amongst a relentless gray flatline, is sated by a constant pushing of your physical ability levels to the point of peril. As skaters we experience this spike nearly every time we leave the house, battling with mental and physical obstructions often for no more than the sake of our own personal enjoyment. Skating Coburg bowl in the scorching afternoon heat with no one else around, I am all too aware that if I somehow knocked myself out then I'd be in that classic Lance Mountain situation where there was a chance of not being found for hours. This attitude, so easily dismissed as idiocy, is what has kept so many of us sane over the years – we have an automatic release valve that the majority of the human race can't even imagine.

50

This release valve is easily vented in my new surroundings, as sprinkled around Melbourne's suburbs are a wide array of skateparks ranging from brand new to dilapidated gnar and from the sublime to the truly abominable. Options aren't limitless, but they are pretty varied; therefore it comes as something of a surprise that the unassuming Fitzroy Bowls have become the epicentre towards which the scene has been inexorably drawn. A small concrete corner of Edinburgh Gardens, with one bizarrely kinked miniature peanut bowl and one bowl descended from three to five feet via a spine and pump bump, it is almost a guarantee that you've been taken here if you've passed through Melbourne with a skateboard. The transitions are lumpy and kinked, the years of paint have made the surface treacherous, the coping has been battered into submission by years of abuse and sounds more like pool than metal coping when a truck locks in, but it still radiates one of the best vibes to be found in the city's many parks.

Fitzroy is an area central to the debates raging, as they are in pretty much every city in the Western world, around Melbourne's gentrification. Once a heavily industrial area, populated by indigenous communities dispossessed from their traditional land as well as a large immigrant population, its proximity to the CBD has seen dramatic rises in rental price markedly change the area's social demographic. Tweely-titled cafes, wine bars populated by sharp-suited city workers, ethnic homogeneity, converted warehouse living arrangements shared with four young professionals who enjoy a glass of wine on the weekend; much as the tides of 'urban regeneration' crash against Brixton's Stockwell Skatepark and it still stands firm, Fitzroy Bowls is unapologetically of the old Melbourne and offers up a much wider (and more interesting) swathe of humanity on a warm Saturday evening than many of the suburb's pubs and bars. In a strange twist on the usual direction of scene cohesion, when talk from the council once turned to funding being allocated to extend the park, the locals joined forces and lobbied against it due to fears that the revamp would up the kook factor to boiling point. The park is a social hub and, even when injured, hours can pass on the bench under the shade of a nearby tree, watching the skating and the patterns of sun spilling through leaves as temporality is warped in clouds of smoke and puddles of spilled beer; taking in the injured, the heatstruck and the mad holding court to a steady background rhythm of urethane on concrete and trucks on coping.

Coburg and Brunswick both boast newer, arguably better skateparks, but I soon come to find that the chances of finding a vibe at either are way lower. Armies of marauding scooter kids, flatground sessions in the bottom of the bowl, coked-up city boys asking for a go on your board while telling you they "used to skate", all of these are much more regular features than at Fitzy. A patch of land in Preston reclaimed by skateboarders and BMXers, christened The Tannery DIY due to the business which used to stand there, becomes my antisocial sanctuary. One evening after a day skating and drinking our way up through the city, the session draws to a close at Brunswick Skatepark. After maybe 20 minutes, I'm approached by Donna; a middle aged woman who asks if I have Instagram. Upon enquiring why, my new friend asks if I could perhaps get a photo taken with her son? Pointing at a bored, pouting teenage boy on a scooter, she tells me that he is an Instagram model with followers; a lot of followers. It would be good for him, she says, to get a photo with someone else at the park, showing what fun we were all having. Her son had decided to relax his facial muscles by this point and was dedicating himself to stroking his carefully coiffed hair, but more than anything, this 'opportunity' would give me some exposure showing people what I did. Unfortunately for Donna, I'm not in the least bit interested in having my photo taken with scooter kids being groomed for a mid-20s mental breakdown. She accepts this with equanimity and shakes my hand, before returning to her son and making him pose for photos until the setting sun captures his features at just the right angle.

Despite her outwardly pleasant demeanour, I am deeply disturbed by the conversation. It always pays to remember that, with skateboarding growing ever more mainstream and being accepted as part of the urban makeup, this is how the majority of people will see us in the future; as sportspeople rather than pests, who do what we do not to feel like we are apart from society but in a desperate plea for acceptance from it. Why wouldn't I want my photo taken with some random teenager, if it was going to gain me wider exposure? Why would I even be skateboarding in the first place? It might be easy for us to laugh at these clueless new additions to skatepark life, but these parents will be raising their children to see skateboarding in the same light as any other cardiovascular activity with a competitive element; something you can, eventually, win at. At that point, we are all fucked.

CHAPTER EIGHT

Urb Ex(crement)

Late one summer's afternoon I leave the house and head up a couple of blocks to Bell Street, the great artery connecting the Northern Suburbs east to west and pulsing with great gouts of commerce, goods and pollution, the traffic thickening into clots then dissipating just enough to allow the freedom to pass through the city without actually seeing any of what may lay beyond the windscreen. A sense of frustration was growing that I wasn't scratching the surface of the city as far as I would have liked and I hoped that a 15km skate to Bulleen Skatepark, followed by a well earned bus journey home, would help. No headphones so my ears could process the endless traffic, the honking horns, the shouted words between acquaintances, anything that may cross my path on this one long push through dead industrial wastelands, existential screams of suburbia, fume-blighted brushland and brief interludes of social and commercial enterprise. Coburg, Preston, Heidelberg, Templestowe; the overlapping suburbs seemed to divide the journey into manageable chunks. The pursuit of my goal (a 70s snake run enriched with some newer concrete additions) was fuelled physically by cans of Melbourne Bitter and Solo, mentally by the desire to explore for which skateboarding is the catalyst for so many. It wasn't until I was about 12 kilometres down that, stopping in a 7/11 to top up my travel card, I realised it was in my other shorts. Full realisation of your own organisational shortcomings is never a pleasant experience, but when it doubles an already cartilage-damaging amount of pushing then the feeling is especially acute.

I went on my first skate trip to Barcelona when I was sixteen and have tried to stay there mentally ever since; the pleasure of discovering a spot known only from videos, the exposure to new people, new places, new experiences, the waft of concrete dust, sweat and beer thickening as the day goes on. It was heartening to realise that, on the other side of the world from where I first rolled around down at the local car park curbs, there was still no end in sight. It's a sure sign that life is going to remain chaotic enough to stay interesting when, at an age when you should really have life's basics dialled to some extent, you're too fried to bring along one of the three items essential to your journey. Skateboarding ended up being my mode of transport for the whole journey, just as it usually is, and the fact that I only skated Bulleen's snake run for half an hour after twenty minutes spent cleaning debris from the deep end was incidental. The camaraderie of a good crew is often essential to what makes skate trips unique, but so sometimes are the lone detours with nothing but your board and a bag on your back. With no good reason other than to see what might be around the next corner, even when the answer seems on the surface to be not much, then the level of communion with your board, your surroundings, their architectural anomalies and the strange behaviour of their denizens negates the possibility of a wasted journey. Maybe it's heatstroke, maybe it's mild carbon monoxide poisoning; but when I get home six hours later, lungs petrol-blackened and feet road-bruised, seething with excitement, I actually feel glad that I forgot my Myki Card. I can't really explain why, but I know that no one asked me to get a photo in pursuit of social media exposure.

In much the same way as regularly touring musicians become better suited to life on the road than off of it, skateboarding too can act as a stimulant for eternal restlessness; a craving for constant motion that makes it hard to stay in one place for a long period of time. After a couple of months in the city, settling into work routines and getting comfortable with the area in which we lived, we headed out to the Dandenong Ranges for a couple of days

55

worth of bush walking. Stopping in the village of Sassafras for a pint, we are devastated to find that its only pub is closed until evening. Thankfully the owner Marco happens to be on the premises, relenting to pouring us a beer on seeing the despondency written clearly on our features by the news. A storm of manic energy, he is conducting a lengthy business discussion on the phone whilst getting our drinks and setting up the bar for the day. Explaining that the nearest open pub is a few kilometres down the road, he offers to drive us down there before taking us on a rally driver's tour of the hairpin curves which make up the Dandenong's roadways. This is accompanied by a stream of consciousness monologue espousing his hatred of city centres, and of London especially, juxtaposed with the peace of mind offered by life in the mountains. I'm finding this peace of mind hard to grasp as we overtake a slow moving vehicle into oncoming traffic ("Bloody tourists can't deal with these roads!"), but when he takes a detour to show us his property I begin to understand. His five acres have been used to build a large, modern house, a separate gym, chicken coops and play areas for his kids, amongst other things, but my mind is wandering back to a trip to Oregon and the various backyard ramps and bowls which I was lucky enough to skate a couple of years before. Thoughts of the skateable terrain that could be built in a property of this size makes a powerful case for putting down roots in the countryside and I think even the most grizzled road warrior would be tempted by the sheer sense of space offered by this spot nestled in the Dandenong foothills, only an hour's drive from Melbourne's CBD.

My own personal picture of Australia growing up, as is arguably the case for most of the Northern Hemisphere, was shaped largely by *Crocodile Dundee*. As such, the impact of where I am hits me hardest during those parts of the trip spent out in the bush, hiking to lookouts and waterfalls, spotting roos and wallabies and experiencing a strange sense of satisfaction whenever we pass a sign warning of snakes. "Melbourne is a great city," people will tell you all over the world, "very European." It is undoubtedly both things; but sometimes it can feel like, in its self-conscious striving to become a metropolitan, cultured Antipodean response to Paris or London, it has lost touch along the way with the rough and ready nature which is such a part of Australia's draw.

After three months without finding a single pub selling stubby coolers, I begin to crave those dusty roadside taverns with sports on the TV, bad mainstream radio on the speakers and cheap schooners for the thirsty traveller. That being said, we catch the Cosmic Psychos one humid Thursday evening in Brunswick and it feels as if all of a sudden we've tapped into a major artery of Australiana; getting in a session at Brunswick clover bowl to start the evening off, with a six pack of lager for dinner followed by a night of songs about tractors, schnitzels and booze, topped off with booze-fuelled breakdancing and fights in the pit? All of a sudden we could be in the depths of rural Queensland rather than a city whose economy seems to be driven by expensive coffee and kombucha, a feeling enhanced when Slim Dusty's 'G'Day, G'Day' plays the band off the stage.

It is an echo of old Melbourne, the gritty, working class Northern Suburbs of the 1980s and '90s when industry still outweighed vintage clothing businesses and the vibrancy of which echoes stronger the further north you head on Sydney Road. This is the point at which the wine bars and vintage stores are replaced by Greek and Lebanese restaurants, shisha bars, mechanics and falafel joints, where a strong immigrant community continues to make its presence felt and the working class vibrancy which once encompassed the majority of the Northern Suburbs still shines through. Just as South London wouldn't be South London without its West Indian flavour, New York wouldn't be New York without Little Italy and Bradford wouldn't be Bradford without its curry houses and mosques, this small stretch of Sydney Road will be much more my abiding memory of Melbourne than the young professional hangouts twenty minutes walk down the strip.

The skate scene is also a reassuringly hard drinking, chain smoking, bad decision making organism thriving on impulse, weed and bottle-o purchases. Skateboarding is in a strange place right now and the position of 'skateboard journalist' is potentially as unsound as it has ever been; the first Olympics to include skateboarding looming, the internet driving a new nail into the coffin of print media with every new social media site to rear its head and, out of the blue, one of the totemic figureheads of our subculture passing away. One of the most noticeable traits about the glut of online obituaries to former *Thrasher* editor Jake Phelps was in relation to how absolutely dedicated he was to skateboarding; whether giving out boards to kids or alienating an entire skate scene with some speed-addled moment of bad behaviour, both light and dark were in some way connected to a plank of wood on wheels. A few people touched on comparisons with Hunter S. Thompson; Phelps' style was rougher, easier to read with semi-amused detachment than the full immersion demanded by Hunter's work, but his embracing of the Gonzo ethos was if anything even more total than that of the Good Doctor. He revelled in an outlaw mythology which he himself helped to build around skateboarding and for many his passing will be the end of an era, another few stones rattled loose in skateboarding's slow landslide from lifestyle to sport.

A couple of days after his passing, two of us with a day off head to a ditch spot in the depths of Fitzroy, battling kinked natural transitions and armies of small but vicious biting ants before hunting down a plaza spot we'd heard rumours of around the corner. It turns out to be almost as rough as the ditch but we get stuck in anyway, starting to get the feel for it when I suddenly notice that the bump I'm attempting to wallride over has a temporary skate stopper; every time I bail out, later and more confidently with each attempt, my board is landing ever closer to a trail of human faeces splattered down the wall and across the landing. It is a timely reminder that, however skateboarding's public face may change in the upcoming years, as long as people are willing to get out of the skatepark and onto the streets then it can never truly be gentrified. Jake Phelps' contribution to skateboarding, and one of the major reasons for the respect he garnered even from those who didn't particularly like him, was that he never once seemed to doubt that.

CHAPTER NINE

DNA on the walls

Although I fall on my feet with regards to the crew I work with, shifts during the summer are thin on the ground (why go to the pub when every park has a free to use BBQ?) so I soon find myself on the hunt for a second job. This search brings me to a seemingly innocent, family-run cake supply warehouse looking for a dishwasher. The last throes of summer have made way for the uncertain birth of a cold, damp autumn and the early morning weather is turning brisk as I push down from Coburg to Collingwood, carving around oil slick puddles and dog turds still glistening with morning dew. The sudden explosion of layers – coats, hats and scarves obscuring faces and features – adds a strange veneer of impersonality to the rush hour bustle until only recently rendered warmer by the ubiquity of tanned skin and vitamin D-enhanced serotonin smiles. Rush hour is always an ugly experience and in the depths of winter its true hideousness is enhanced tenfold, but for now the full scope of anxiety – that which can emanate from a society in the grip of the knowledge that they will both enter and leave their concrete and glass prisons without seeing daylight – is yet to be realised. The sun will have burnt off the morning chill by midday, the nights have yet to draw in and hopelessness has not yet taken hold, so I'm feeling confident that by late afternoon I'll be parked up at a skatepark with another job to see me through the upcoming months.

I am welcomed into the building by the owner's son, a tall, stooped man with an air of distraction about him. He points me in the direction of an industrial-sized sink surrounded by a teetering pile of dirty baking equipment and explains vaguely that their previous washer 'disappeared' a week or two previously. I am given an apron and the most urgent piles of washing but no further instructions before he scurries into an office at the back of the building, so I'm left to annoy the floor staff for further instructions. The further I progress through layers of tubs, pots, baking trays and whisks, the thicker the air becomes with backspray from the tap and, increasingly, a variety of moulds which quickly coat my apron, glasses and face with a filthy, glutinous paste. Being British means that the only way I can start conversations with people is by mentioning the weather, so I attempt to distract myself from potential permanent lung damage by stating what a nice day it is outside to a woman of indeterminate middle age. This elicits a chuckle; "Hot, cold, dry, rain, none of it matters for us in here!" Said with a sweet smile, it is seemingly meant as a positive statement but instead fills me with an overwhelming sense of dread.

By the time the owner – a malignant, bearded gnome of a man with milk bottle glasses and no regard for personal space – enters the building around midday, I have already decided not to take the job. Before I can bring this up he tells me that he is happy to give me the role sight unseen before leaning conspiratorially closer to my face; "The thing is, I've had trouble with all these Asians, sneaking around working one day or week then quitting and only returning to collect their pay. I can tell you're trustworthy, but if you ever try to fuck me over then believe me, I'll already be one step ahead of you." I accept the fact that, now, I have to work a full day before quitting and only returning to collect my pay; something in my psyche delights in seeing how far I can push people I take a dislike to. A combination of stupidity and aggressiveness tinged with racist overtones makes this guy a prime candidate for someone I'd like to nudge towards a rage-induced brain haemorrhage. Four o'clock comes around and I remove my apron, telling the younger owner that I am done. "Okay, so we can get you in tomorrow..." "I don't think this job is for me," I cut him off. After waiting for a couple of minutes to enjoy the elder's reaction, which is suitably apoplectic, I head to Edinburgh Gardens. It is time for a well-earned skate and a beer, hat firmly tipped to Charles Bukowski as I contemplate the shortest job I ever had.

With a work pattern thus still limited to a couple of pub shifts a week, Melbourne's wide array of skateable delights still take up the majority of my time. A small crew of us take to regular weekend missions across the city and surrounding areas, eating up the kilometres to hit terrain ranging from brand new skateparks to venerable concrete dinosaurs (Corio's cheese grater surface means you're only ever one slam away from needing a skin graft) and from marble plazas to crumbling brick U-pipes. Nestled in almost the dead centre of Port Phillip Bay, Melbourne's suburbs stretch like the pincers of a crab towards the Mornington Peninsula in the east and Geelong in the west. Both pincers have their own charms when it comes to rideable architecture, whilst the depths of the Northern Suburbs are similarly littered with prime industrial wasteland and half forgotten concrete pits; sacrificial altars to the skate gods to which we play the part of willing victims. The city's suburbs sprawl for miles and you don't need to head for the hinterlands before things start to take on a much more 'small town' vibe; half of the skaters we talk to in city's central parks have never even heard of Epping or Greensborough, each only a 25 minute drive from Fitzroy, let alone skated there. This disinterest from the central Melbourne skate scene makes for a fertile breeding ground for the outcast/mosher end of the skate spectrum.

Almost no distance at all from the self conscious posing of the teenagers skating Riverslide, you find yourself in the realms of skintight jeans, Deicide t-shirts and roastbeef flyouts. It might be stylistically questionable, but when you've grown up as a small town weirdo then there's something indelibly comforting about finding these eccentric bastions of nerdiness so close to a metropolitan hub.

Melbourne is ridiculously well equipped with a wide array of skateparks but, as the pleasures of the purpose-built spot begin to pall, we find ourselves on ever-increased alertness for a rougher, grimmer, realer session. This sees us hitting the road at least once a week, obsessively picking through the industrial detritus of late 20th century capitalism, revelling in the landscape against which the slow decline of Western society is played out. Each abandoned factory, each empty pool, each dead patch of land speaks of jobs lost, of bankruptcy, of personal dreams abandoned on the scrap heap of life. These abandoned dreams become our playground as, vulture-like, we circle above via Google Earth or word of mouth awaiting the chance to pounce. And, much as vultures are integral to the ecosystem of which they are a part, the use we put these dead zones to is much more life affirming than the land being flattened to make way for another multinational supermarket chain or luxury housing for the wealthy elite.

Occasionally the stories behind these spots have less depth; my first Australian backyard pool is one we spot on a friend's social media account and finds us at a house party in one of Melbourne's more affluent suburbs. The origins of the modern swimming pool, so deeply imbedded in skateboarding's subconscious, can be found not in some sun drenched corner of the USA but rather unexpectedly in the icy rural hinterlands of Finland circa 1938 – where architect Alvar Aalto's designs for the Villa Mairea, a building iconic in architectural circles, included amongst its unconventional concepts a unique swimming pool. Unlike the square swimming pool design which was standard for the time, the pool featured a gradient from 'shallow' to 'deep' end; both shallow and deep saw the flat bottom transition to the wall in a steep curve rather than a 90 degree angle, creating a bowled out effect. The impact that this aesthetic development would have on skateboarding would be immeasurable. The shape of the pool itself, seen from above, looked like a kidney bean.

Aalto's Villa was made possible by the patronage of Harry and Maire Gullischen, who saw in increased industrialisation a utopian future and whose vision was one in which everyone would have the means to visit upscale rural retreats such as the Villa Mairea. Whether or not they would appreciate the irony of the abandoned pool, against a backdrop of societal and industrial decline, becoming such an archetypal image within skate culture – or indeed enjoy the unintended use to which skateboarders have put them – is something no one thought to ask them.

What is known is that, nine years after the Villa's completion in 1948, a similar-shaped pool built in California grabbed the attention of the upper classes and became the garden feature de rigeur. For nearly three decades pools based on Aalto's concept were built across the US, when in 1975 the US West Coast was struck by a drought which saw homeowners leaving their status symbols high and dry. This just happened to coincide with the rise of the skateboard as a pastime for bored surfers when the swell was mild, and these pools (alongside the mellower, easier to ride curves of Californian schoolyard slopes) quickly became the go-to fix when surf was unavailable. Pools were the birthing place of many of the tricks, stylistic quirks and cultural tropes which still govern skateboarding today, and for someone raised in the decidedly backyard pool-free confines of East Sussex they are pretty much the holy grail.

Despite its climate, backyard swimming pools featuring curves are an anomaly on Australia's lower East Coast – the high prevalence of sand in Western Australia makes for a more stable soil in which to build round pools, giving them the monopoly. Meanwhile the unstable ground below Melbourne and Sydney, littered with bluestone, means that the stronger square pool is a much safer proposition. Even so attempts have been made in Melbourne, with varying degrees of success, to pay respects to Aalto's legacy. This leads us to the aforementioned house party thrown by a group of snowboarders who, with their lease running out, decided it was finally time to drain out the pit in their garden and swap powder for concrete. The Saturday in question comes around cloaked in a thick drizzle, but it'll take more than that to deter us and we persevere with a warm up at the nearby Clayton Skatepark with the aid of a broom borrowed from the adjacent bowls club to dry the park up; "You lot are eager, aren't you?" sums up the bartender. The sun eventually turtleheads its way through the clouds but the rain remains imminent, so we make sure to stock up on booze between park and party in case the pool is a washout. Thankfully it isn't, with a huge tarp erected by the residents to keep the pool (and DJ setup above the deep end) dry, but the transition itself is way gnarlier than any of us had imagined.

The amount of vert in the deep makes anything more than a few carves unlikely, while the only place the shallow end can realistically be hit is via a foot wide scoop of hastily added concrete. This curves about two feet up the wall before a solid two foot of vert, with the pour already starting to crack at the base. Nonetheless a bunch of people are getting stuck in, hitting the back wall as high as possible, testing out various mosher drop possibilities and trying not to terminally damage too much ankle cartilage on the DIY 'crete in the shallow. A rolling cast of skaters are gradually thinned out by slams, mind-altering substances and combinations of the two, but not before a couple of tricks are somehow rolled away from. Eventually a fine sheen of drizzle brought in on the wind slowly turns the pool's tiles into an icy death trap. The craic is still high, with pure adrenaline being channelled straight from the skate into the party, but the inevitable crash starts to come and we head out in order to avoid waking up hungover on someone's floor halfway to the Mornington Peninsula.

A few days later, we're sorting weekend plans when word starts filtering down of another backyard pit laying dormant behind a motel in Coburg. Clearly not one of Melbourne's classier establishments, the first review on TripAdvisor reads like the junk-dream poetic ravings of a second rate Burroughs;

"Terrible hotel, don't stay here
It's filthy dirty. There are holes punched in the inside door
Tiles all broken in the bathroom
The whole Place stinks of urine
DNA on the walls, Wiring hanging out of the wall
Bed cover had cigarette burn holes, windows wouldn't close
Grubby little man running the place, would not come
and show me how to get into the room.
Took my money quickly and gave no customer service at all
An embarrassment to Melbourne, should be demolished."

Further reviews detail empty Jim Beam cans littering reception, stairwells piled high with fragrant rubbish bags, mouldy fridges and a 'green and filthy' swimming pool. It was this green and filthy water we found ourselves ankle deep in one grey Sunday afternoon after another on/off shower warm up at Coburg Skatepark's kidney bowl, bailing out litres of slime with buckets and praying that the pregnant clouds building overhead held off for at least a few more hours. I guess this was technically another permission pool as, despite various staff members going about their duties on the grounds, none of them even batted an eyelid at six skateboarders industriously bailing out stagnant water from their pool and pouring it into the grass. They didn't even have anything to say when the sounds of screeching urethane filled the air. The pool itself was, if anything, even harder to skate than the previous week's; no shallow end to speak of, just a short run up from the steps before jumping on, powering through the elbow pocket and then hitting a deep end seemingly modelled on a fifty pence piece. The dead centre of the deep was nearly, but not quite, transitioned enough to be skateable, while further around the side walls it turned into something like a giant jersey barrier. After all that draining we weren't going to let something minor like the fact that the spot was shit get in our way and a heavy carve session soon got going, with coping in the deep end eventually scratched by sundown.

Pool number three, its address gleaned from a drunken evening on Fitzroy Skatepark's bench, turns out to be the best of the lot; deeper than the Coburg pit and with more vert, but with a much smoother transition. It still isn't perfect – carving over the light takes the majority of us a good portion of the session and it isn't until the second visit that anyone hits coping – but it probably does the most of all three for lighting a fire and kicking off the hunt for backyard pools and rugged street transitions which follows.

The following weekend we don't find pool number four, but we do manage to sneak into the legendary Bluestone DIY between the asbestos removal team and the demolition crew. We'd tried a week or so before and been turned back by workers, who had given us fairly concrete dates of when was a good time to return; so, despite the fine layer of almost certainly lung damaging dust which coated the spot when we finally hopped the fence, a heavy session saw numerous tricks documented in both film and photo form. Coming as it did on top of regular sessions at Preston DIY, the site of a former tannery where any kind of legitimate building work has been hindered by high levels of arsenic in the ground, it probably did nothing for our physical longevity. But, then, what's a few blood-splattered coughing fits among friends? The Doomsday Clock is once again toying with ticking over to midnight so we might as well go and roll around in antique insulation with our friends in the hope that skate travel publications are below the radar of life insurance companies.

I eventually start to pick up a few extra shifts once flu season comes around by dint of a share-house-hardened immune system. I have developed a few pet theories about why a lot of skaters rarely come down with cold and flu bugs and at the top of these has to be long term exposure to skate houses and the questionable hygiene often found within. Many years of sharing living quarters with people who would much rather head to the nearest miniramp than wipe down a stove top has turned my white blood cells into battle-scarred veterans of multiple wars. Not that I'm at a loss when flu symptoms do start manifesting themselves, with a three step plan in my arsenal that rarely fails:

Step 1, go out and skate wearing as many layers as possible. This should help sweat out most of the germs pretty fast. Step 2, cook all meals with chillies, ginger and garlic, alongside a generous helping of dark greens. Never underestimate the power of a good feed. Step 3, if steps 1 and 2 have failed – go buy a big bottle of whiskey, get fucking faded. This should obliterate nearly any germ which has had the temerity to enter your body and not be shifted by steps 1 and 2.

This faintly ludicrous combination of healthy living and alcoholic folk remedies with no medical basis keeps me healthy enough to cover most of those shifts left by sneezing, shaking colleagues and hone my ability to fake an in-depth knowledge of the world of craft beer. Craft brewing has enjoyed a strange renaissance in the last few years. What was once the jealously-guarded realm of the CAMRA snob, with its ins and outs used solely by middle-aged men who smelled like egg and cress sandwiches to bore younger people with at the bar, has been democratised; now young and old, male or female, waft of stale egg or nay, a wide swathe of society are determined to bore you at the bar with discussions about mouthfeel, citrus flavours or why you're wrong for buying a pint of lager.

The pub I end up employed in is nice, I get on with my colleagues, but unfortunately it's on the frontline of the craft beer revival so I'm regularly forced into discussions about the relative merits of different IPAs when I'd rather have a four pack of Holsten Pils. Our taps come with handy notes on the back for when the management accidentally employ philistines like me, which makes things much easier and offers an outlet for one manager's Viz-like sense of humour; one particularly popular pale ale being memorably described as having a "silky, protein-laden mouthfeel." I spend some time toying with the idea of trying to say those words to a customer with a straight face, but realise that I don't want to leave the country on some kind of register.

One night after work we end up sinking a few beers in the back in the midst of a hectic weekend and 3am finds me bombing the few hills near my house. The lights of a thousand houses open up before me as I hit the top of Mitchell Parade and life's possibilities seem endless as the incline increases and I feel my bearing cases rattling ever faster. I can't reconcile the beauty before me with the decisions that some people make to finish their own lives, I can barely even type this without getting confused and upset; it makes me wonder what I missed, how I could have helped in some way but somehow didn't. Sitting numbly on the sofa on the first night after the news, watching as much of Ben's prodigious visual output as we can find, my initial feelings of devastation are intertwined with an appreciation of the community we are a part of. This is one of the saddest days of my life, but intermingling with the tears is the happiness I can take from knowing that Ben, and so many other incredible humans, have found their way into my life because of skateboarding. About two weeks before we left for the Southern Hemisphere, Ben rang me to see if I wanted to go on a five day skate trip somewhere around the south, which I obviously turned down. It took some explaining as to why I couldn't go, what with all the packing boxes, last minute organisation and all the admin nausea that comes with moving abroad, and I'm not sure he quite realised how unlikely it was for me to make it on his trip – that was just the way he was, unconcerned about the practicalities of day to day living. That's not necessarily a bad thing and, despite the sheer unlikeliness of my being able to join that particular trip, I will now forever regret not saying "Fuck it" and going for it.

CHAPTER TEN

No beer on a dead planet

One of the unexpected bonuses of extended travel is the sense of dislocation from world events; political upheaval in your parent country can seem incredibly distant, while closer events are rendered opaque by dint of your status as tourist rather than citizen. This is the situation I find myself in during the 2019 Australian elections, feeling vaguely guilty about how much I'm enjoying not giving a fuck about them due to my semi-transient condition. Despite my disengagement from the Australian political machine, it doesn't take much of an interest to realise what a disaster the ensuing result is for a country whose major claim to fame is its position under a man-made prolapse in the ozone layer. A victory for the Liberal-National Coalition and Scott Morrison is a result whose origins are pretty unclear if you don't have at least a basic degree in Machiavellian politics but, if the whisperings from the heartlands are to be believed, his seat is in no danger for a long time.

In fact in two hundred years, the planet ravaged by superstrength UV rays and freak natural disasters, on a small patch of liveable Australian soil, the nation's longest running PM will once again be up for re-election. His followers, enjoying a respite from vicious running battles with the gruesomely mutated descendents of Pauline Hansen's inbred disciples, will look up from their meals of nuclear effluent and long pig as the long-serving man of the people stands proud atop a mound of charred skulls. Flesh and bone long replaced by a titanium exoskeleton impervious to melanoma, acid rain and carcinogenic fumes on the wind, the relentless sun will glint sharply off of Morrison's robotic fist as it holds aloft a crumbling lump of coal and his ragged cohort look on in awe. "Don't be afraid," he will say, "Don't be scared."

Much as with other populist political victories across the globe in recent years, the Coalition's win has been met with much public outcry and strongly voiced fears for the future – in this case not just for the country over the next few years, but for the long term prospects of the earth itself. This is something we find starkly worded as we reach Hobart's city centre just after dawn, with "No beer on a dead planet" scrawled in bold lettering on a pub blackboard. It is a sobering thought at 7am on a cold Tasmanian morning, one which is brought back more strongly with each ever-more-beguiling view that the state offers up over the course of the following week. Tasmania's natural sights seem such primordial and eternally enduring vistas that it is hard to picture the hand of man having much impact, but it doesn't take much consideration of Great Barrier Reefs and whatnot to realise that this is not the case. It is sunny when we first begin our week of travelling in Australia's southernmost state, but by the time we have breakfast and check into our hotel then Tasmania's notoriously dodgy weather has taken hold and a thick drizzle shows little sign of letting up for the day.

A visit to Hobart's Salamanca Markets yield up some high strength cider which we put aside for an evening looking increasingly likely to be spent indoors and, with the city's outdoor activities obscured by sheets of precipitation, we head to the harbourside to catch a ferry to the Museum of Old and New Art. The ride takes in the meanderings of the River Derwent through Hobart's industrial suburbs, rising dystopian and stark from the shoreline, before stopping off at a small outcrop of land which houses what owner David Walsh has called a "subversive adult Disneyland." Whether it matches that level of hyperbole is open to interpretation, but regardless it is an interestingly irreverent collection of artworks in a truly impressive darkly-lit dungeon of a building, its ambience well matched by the driving rain and slate grey skies outside. Once we've had our fill of Walsh's collection (apparently a labour of love operation which loses way more than it makes, so fair play to him), our years of training for this sort of weather come into play and we head straight from the return ferry into a pub, followed at length by another pub. Weather conditions here aren't far removed from those in the UK and, accordingly, the drinking establishments which litter Hobart's harbour are warm, welcoming retreats from the elements. Even the names are redolent of coastal Britain – *The Whaler, The Custom House, The Hope and Anchor* – and, as with UK venues, at least one pub dinner is a must when visiting the town. Hobart was, in fact, the birthplace of Australia's first cookbook. *The English and Australian Cookery Book: Cooking for the Many, as well as the Upper Ten Thousand* was first published in 1864 by Edward Abbott, a deputy judge advocate posted from New South Wales to Tasmania in 1815. The book runs to nearly 300 pages and includes chapters on coffee and tea, alcoholic drinks, eggs, fish, game, dessert and more. Recipes, meanwhile, include 'Slippery Bob' – Edward's own recipe for kangaroo brains fried in emu fat. Discovering this fact on a plinth in the city earlier in the day, we scan a few menus in vain for the dish before sadly having to settle on burgers. Fuelled up, we head back to our hotel to get acquainted with the strong cider, which coupled with our eighteen hour day on top of three hours of sleep puts us under in minutes.

The next day, definitely not replenished but definitely not quite as frazzled as the day before, we head downstairs to take advantage of the complimentary breakfast. The excitable receptionist is hyped to find out that I am a skateboarder and conversation quickly turns to the respective merits of Peter Smolik, Stevie Williams and the Osiris D3. On a tiny, rainswept island on the other side of the world from your family and friends, running mostly on caffeine fumes mixed with the remnants of the previous night's cider binge, this sort of connection does wonders for getting your day started. We leave him with promises of switch hardflips that I have no plans of fulfilling and head out into the sun. Our plan is to get some breakfast then head up to the concrete dinosaur that sits atop the hills of West Hobart, having a skate for Ben in lieu of us being able to make his funeral. After that, a bus will take us up to the base of Mount Wellington before we hike the rest of the way and scope out a potential skate spot which is formed by the roof of the shelter at the mountain's summit. Being Tasmania the weather has other plans and between leaving the hotel and reaching the snake run at the top of West Hobart's steep, winding hills, two heavy showers have left the park treacherously slick. Heading back down defeated, we clock another slightly less damp skatepark at the bottom of the hill and a few frontside grinds are battled through the puddles. After lunch the park is nearly dry, while Mount Wellington is looking like an unpleasantly bleak prospect judging by the handicam footage conveniently running on a local website, so we switch up our plans yet again. We find out from a local ripper called Danny that the top of the mountain is often closed in bad weather so settle in for an afternoon in the city's lower climes. We even give the snake run another shot, finding it still moist but cleared up enough for a few slash grinds. A second roll at the park down the hill sees the weather finally catching up to us, sending us scurrying to the shelter of various pubs for the rest of the evening now safe in the knowledge that we'd done Ben proud.

After a final morning in Hobart checking out Kangaroo Bay skatepark and its incredible kidney pool we hit the road for Freycinet National Park – a spot recommended by nearly everyone who we'd spoken to about visiting the state beforehand. We were also warned by many about watching out for wildlife on the roads around dusk, something which I hadn't quite believed could live up to the hype despite the impressive amounts of roadkill piled on the side of the road being picked at by murder upon murder of sleek, well-fed crows. The first few critters start appearing just as the sun hits the horizon and, as night truly falls, wallabies are hopping into the path of our high beams like lemmings towards the cliff edge; if anything, the situation was undersold to us. The size of the crows here begins to make sense as the last hour of driving becomes a tense marsupial slalom course, and I reach Coles Bay very ready for a celebratory pint to mark my lack of dented front bumper or bad karma points. We head to the only pub in town, getting in at about half seven and finding out that we have an hour's drinking time before last orders. The barman shrugs philosophically; "Quiet town, quiet season, quiet state." You get the feeling that the quiet season is the main reason for the early close, as this town is the gateway to one of Tasmania's most celebrated beaches in Wineglass Bay. We had planned to take in this sight from the top of Mount Amos – one of the three imposing rock formations collectively known as The Hazards which jut out of Freycinet's forest canopy and dominate the surrounding landscape – but hadn't factored in the need for footwear more sturdy than a pair of battered skate shoes, so settle for the regular tourist hike instead.

At a different time of year this would most likely have been packed; but, while there were a few selfie-stick-laden tourists at the peak of the walk, not many opt for the final leg of the journey down to the bay itself. After a short, steep climb we end up with a curving stretch of white sand shared between ourselves and one other person, who after a few minutes departs to leave us with a truly breathtaking view to ourselves. This is the first time we put our finger on what seems so unique about Tasmanian beaches – the lack of plastic washing up on the shore. The same goes for the countryside; no discarded soft drink bottles or McDonalds wrappers, no plastic packaging trundling along in the breeze. Whether this is due to the state's small population or a genuine effort by residents to completely clean up after themselves is not for me to say, but optimism makes me wish for the latter. Having skipped the mountain climb, we also establish that Vans are not built for 15km round trips and head home for an early night (not that there are many options for a late one around here) and the promise of minimal walking the following day.

This starts with breakfast down by the water with once again not another tourist in sight, despite sweeping views across the bay and a steadily climbing sun taking the edge off of Antarctic winds. A couple of curious seagulls approach in the hope of food, but even these are small, cute, gleamingly clean artistic details in the frame – very distant cousins to the wiry, violent scavengers that menace holiday goers in towns like Brighton and Scarborough, fired up on a combination of steroids and methamphetamines as they swarm anyone or anything at the mere hint of deep fried potato. Even the larger Pacific Gulls make their regal way across the sands, not deigning to anything so base as beg humans for scraps.

Other than Hobart and Launceston, Tasmanian civilisation consists exclusively of small towns geared towards the tourist season so our trip up the coast is based around such wholesome fresh air activities as bushwalking and wildlife spotting. Seals frolic in the shallows at Bicheno and tame wallabies hop unconcerned alongside tourists in Freycinet, but it is a carelessly discarded bucket of fish guts that afford us the most rewarding encounter of the trip with Tasman fauna. Heading to the harbour at Bay of Fires to watch the sun set, we find ourselves instead transfixed by the animal kingdom's hierarchy with regards to who gets first dibs on such a feast. Two pelicans are the first in, lancing their beaks into the oily mess and sending arcs of stringy fish innards gleaming into the air as they gulp it down their throats. Underneath the surface a couple of reef sharks start in on what the pelicans haven't decimated, whilst seagulls and other other small birds are left impatiently waiting for whatever is left behind at the end. After a quarter of an hour watching this strange pantomime, a huge dark shape glides into view, hugging the sea bed; a shape which solidifies itself on closer inspection into a mammoth stingray, a regular sight at this spot according to a passing local dog walker.

Sitting by the water, with the sun splashing its spectacular palette across the sky, it's hard to picture the near-relentless downpour which accompanied our time in Hobart. We didn't even get the worst of it; an older woman taking in the view with her husband, clearly thinking along the same lines, gets her phone out to show us footage of their car being pushed out of a snow drift on Cradle Mountain only the previous week.

The next morning after breakfast, we start the car and head towards one of the most important milestones of the trip; in the hamlet of Pyengana, deep in the brilliantly named Break O'Day municipality, lies the Pub in the Paddock. Despite it's truly idyllic surroundings and cosy countryside pub interior, its true draw lies in one particular local barfly – Priscilla, a resident of the adjacent pig farm, who has picked up a taste for the hard stuff. You could be a farmer just finished for the day and stopping for a cold one after work and, whether the pub had any other human customers or not, be guaranteed a drinking buddy. It's around 10am when we stop through and as I still have a mountainous drive through to

Launceston I don't get to share a beer with a pig, but we do stop to pay our respects to Priscilla and her neighbours before driving slightly further down the road to the secluded St Columba Falls. The falls are either 'Tasmania's highest waterfall' or 'One of Tasmania's highest waterfalls' depending on which source you come across (upon further research, the record belongs to Montezuma Falls, near Rosebery on the island's West Coast), but either way it's a stunning place to stop and stretch your legs after putting in some time on the road.

From here we continue on towards Launceston, a breathtaking drive of winding mountain roads, sweeping views and frankly terrifying gorges only inches from the edge of the tarmac. Add in a few hairpin turns along the way and I don't find myself taking this part of the journey at much speed, much to the irritation of various four wheel drive owners as well as the group of expensive car enthusiasts who had been stopping for refreshments in Pyengana as we left. If I'm honest I find the sight of this lot tailing me as I potter along in a rented Hyundai fairly amusing, but I'm less complacent when it comes to Landrovers and Utes. It would only take one disgruntled farmer – misanthropically twisted by years of getting stuck behind tourist drivers and reckless from matching Priscilla beer for beer at breakfast – to reach boiling point, and we would be only so much roadkill in the valley below. Luckily we manage to avoid any confrontation with murderous, pig drunk rednecks and arrive at Launceston at dusk unscathed and ready to get into some serious pint necking. Launceston is in a sense the Canberra of Tasmania, spoken of in scathing terms by visitors and residents of other parts of the state alike, but our admittedly fleeting 24 hour visit offered it in a different light; a small industrial town, undoubtedly not conventionally pretty, which still offered up bush hikes within a fifteen minute walk of the city centre (not something you'd find in most cities), friendly drinking establishments and a pleasantly archaic, characterful skatepark.

We wake up to a thick fog blanketing the town and rendering it invisible from our window, but this begins to lift as we meander along the riverbank dodging the splattered stomach chunk street portrait remnants of the previous night's festivities. Arriving at a skatepark which is both still damp from the receding fog and simultaneously heaving with scooter kids, we decide to head across to Cataract Gorge despite the temptation to watch to its inevitable horrific denouement the group of kids daring each other to ride down a steep tarmac berm in a stolen supermarket trolley. This turns out to be a stunning trail winding along the South Esk river, bordered by sedately moving water on one side and a near sheer rock face on the other. Aboriginal lore tells how the boulders which line the gorge are ancestors transformed into stone to stand guard and care for the area. The route is studded with viewing huts, recreated from the original Victorian shelters long since collapsed and offering an insight into the psyche of those early European settlers who longed to bring some sense of order to the beautifully chaotic whims of nature. This reaches its apex at the Cliff Grounds, a manicured Victorian Garden complete with lawns, a swimming pool and peacocks (fucking peacocks!) in the shadow of the gorge walls. This jarring sight, the hand of man painting over nature's canvas, is so incongruous the mind can only accept it in sci-fi terms; humanity attempting to terraform Mars after earth has been beaten into a rotting refuse pile, a garbage steamer floating through time and space with the raving Australian PM at its helm, ScomEarth realised with all its concomitant repercussions.

CHAPTER ELEVEN

Myths, nomads and cicadas

It is an implausibly dry, still winter's evening and the steadily darkening sky over the Eastern Suburbs is holding its breath as we attempt to grasp a skate session from the jaws of the inevitable exhale. Harsh flood lighting illuminates the undulating concrete curves of Noble Skatepark, dulled in the return glint from scores of half-drunk beer bottles but throwing everything else into stark relief; the lines of cold and Vitamin D deficiency etched into skaters' features, the lacquer glistening from pits and chunks in the well-worn pool coping, every millimetre of the delicate wing pattern belonging to a cicada limping on a meandering course guided by its subconscious. The unnatural fold which mars one wing and the incongruous sight of a missing leg categorises this course as a testament to, and result of, some primal survival urge. Scientists in recent years have put forward the theory that cicadas are evolving to only emerge in cycles based around prime numbers, putting them outside of the realm of predator population cycles and allowing their numbers to flourish. In this sorry specimen, a microcosm of its entire species' survival mechanism can be seen; but, it is probably safe to say, the latter will be more successful than the former. This does not deter the owner of the work-lined, suntanned hand which gently scoops the broken creature from its allotted course.

Noble is one of the best and most recognisable bowls in the Melbourne area, with its huge pool coping bowl playing host to the King of Concrete jam every year. Chuck in an extensive street course, a lengthy snake run and a nearby bottle-o that sells long necks of Phoenix (the "Famous Beer of Mauritius") cheaper than most places in the city, and you have a park which draws in daily an array of out-of-towners and skate tourists. Lisa, injured insect cradled in palm with a skateboard for the moment forgotten, is one of the more intriguing of these visitors. Cruising about the park in mismatched slides (Australian slang for plastic sandals) would normally be the reserve of mongo pushers and longboarding beach bums, but Lisa has been taking the griptape pedicure approach with 360 flips stomped up the Wembley Gap all evening. With origins in Nimbin and a current home in a camper van parked around the corner, Noble is a pit stop on the endless road which exerts an implacable pull on so many Australians both natural and naturalized.

The rain is threatening to end the night's skating as big, irregular drops start to hit the concrete, but right now the cicada is Lisa's main focus as the pros and cons of different adhesives and their likelihood of fixing damaged insect parts are methodically weighed up. Debating the superiority of superglue or sellotape in terms of whether it will hold a cicada together gives the evening a strangely dreamlike, abstract quality. When the weather finally sends us scurrying for our vehicles Lisa disappears into the night, cicada clutched in hand, a dreadlocked Siddhartha searching for their river.

The tail end of winter in Melbourne moves at a slower pace than the warmer months, with both routine and weather threatening to dampen the search for concrete flagellation, but these chance meetings enliven the seasonal monotony and help remind me why I am here. Even so, the events which the writer can make seem almost mythological on paper in reality feel insignificant at the time; the angry looking bald man in front of me in the bottle shop queue, mall grabbing a RAW Rizla complete skateboard set up (including matching grip art), who refuses to acknowledge my skateboard or friendly nod; the gnome-like elderly woman who sits in the back room of the pub shouting 'go away' repeatedly at a group of yuppies but calms down once I sit with her so she can tell me about the visions and characters she can see flickering in the fireplace; the wet days looking for dry spots, the group chats deciphering the forecast, the rained-off sessions, the ones snatched from the jaws of drizzling defeat, the drunken nights, the psilocybin adventures, joints shared on the skatepark bench, endless beers – Melbourne Bitter, Victoria Bitter, Furphy Refreshing Ale, Cooper's Pale, Mountain Goat, all different labels for the self-destructive fashion in which we deal with the winter blues. We skate when it's dry, we practice patience when it isn't, our chance encounters are as much with the nomadic spirits of our own subconscious as with flesh and blood. Just as the clouds start to clear and the temperatures start pushing past 20 degrees Celsius, we masochistically chase the cold by hopping on a flight over to Queenstown, nestled deep within the mountains on New Zealand's South Island.

Getting to Melbourne's Tullamarine Airport, we hit our first snag. The woman working the desk at check-in tells me that getting into New Zealand is impossible without a return visa for another country, and as such I won't be allowed into the country until my new Australian visa is sorted. Of course, you can't apply for an Australian visa while you are in the country itself. This bizarre Catch 22 results in me having to book a flight to Fiji, which I then cancel once in New Zealand before booking my return visa for Australia. This leaves me $100 poorer and 100% more stressed out than the damage already wrought by work and sleep deprivation. At least, however, we are on a plane; one which, against the odds, arrives at Queenstown Airport in glorious sunshine. Attempts to caffeinate myself back into reality fall short, but the first sight of Queenstown Gardens Bowl does wonders. A snowman-shaped bowl with a ten-foot deep end, six-foot shallow, an extra whippy pocket at one end for good measure and chunky bullnose pool coping is ideal for blasting through the cobwebs – especially once a few slams have been dispensed. It's the closest thing I've skated so far in the Southern Hemisphere to a Dreamlands skatepark and, with my wobbly plane legs not at their finest, I am determined to come back before I leave.

For now though, suitably bloodied and alert, I meet Alyce for a sunset walk through an area almost fairytale in appearance. Pine growth reaches down towards the water, hemmed in on other shores by distant snow-capped peaks, and broken by shards of sunlight bouncing incandescent and beguiling into the ether. Lovers stroll across the stones, bird call is rife through the twilight air, and so are the frisbees. Yep, frisbees. I'm not sure what we have wandered into, but at least 20 people are walking amongst the trees involved in some form of incomprehensible game. It does nothing for the serenity of the moment, so rather than enquire further we make a beeline for the Irish pub by the waterfront and sip a couple of pints to the classic Celtic sounds of The Pogues, Christy Moore and – for some reason known only to the bar staff and perhaps the frisbee players – Sublime. I'm sure that somewhere, some unrecognised genius has sheaves of documents explaining the connection between frisbee players and Sublime, but without those to hand I can only say that my subconscious files them close to each other, in the thick folder labelled 'mildly irritating'. The connection between Sublime and the Emerald Isle, however, has yet to be established. The next day another clear, sunny morning by the waterfront further cements my opinion that Queenstown operates in its own bizarre musical dimension, as we pass a grizzled old busker and his large bearded collie performing a duet of 'House of the Rising Sun'. I'm happy to say that what the dog lacked in ability to keep tune, it more than made up for in enthusiasm.

A bus ride through rolling hills and deeply shaded valleys brings us to Arrowtown, a village only a short drive from Queenstown which is home to an incredible historic site. About a third of the place is taken up by a restored Chinese mining village, which tells the story of these gold rush immigrants via plaques dotted amongst tiny huts built in the shadow of the adjacent rock face and even hewn from the rock itself. The area has been historically characterised by the pursuit of riches – Maoris knew the area for its abundance of the highly valued 'pounamu' or 'greenstone' – and it was the discovery of gold in the Arrow River in 1862 which drew many Europeans to the area. In the mid 1860s the opening of more fruitful goldfields saw many settlers depart and the economy begin to flag, at which point local authorities invited Chinese miners in an attempt to revive the area's fortunes.

The day is still bright and children run amongst the huts and down by the banks of the Arrow River, but the ingrained presence of these men and the predicament they faced upon arrival leaves a chill; lodging in cramped quarters thousands of miles from family and home, facing not just harsh winters but also the extreme racism of the European settlers – a discriminatory poll tax on Chinese immigrants was not repealed until 1944 and a number of anti-Asian groups thrived in the late 19th and early 20th centuries. It wouldn't be too long before we would witness the remaining traces of this bigotry in the flesh.

For now, however – after a beer in the sun only slightly marred by an obnoxious Scottish backpacker on the next table regaling his friends (or captives) with a ranking of 'countries to smoke weed in' on a scale ranging from 'loose' to 'really not loose' – we head back to Queenstown and another round at the skatepark. We are joined by a French couple who are just learning to skate and are keen to share some hash and find out more about what is in store. "Tell me," asks one apprehensively, leaning in through a cloud of smoke, "...are all bowls this hard to use?" I assure him that after this most bowls will feel like a breeze, though if their next stop happens to be Wanaka I would almost definitely be cursed as a liar. Wanaka is, in fact, our next stop in the morning, after a coffee down by the shores of Lake Wakatipu. Sitting next to such a large body of water as it does, it is unsurprising that the town is home to plenty of water-based activities. These range from jet skis, to scenic ferry trips, to a mini-submarine painted like a shark which we see periodically emerging from the water. As we wait for our coffee, a woman sitting at the next table with her family jumps out of her seat and waves a hand frantically towards the water; "Oh my god, look everyone – a killer whale just breached!" The colour drains from her face as a nearby waitress points out the submarine-esque cast of her Orca, her kids cringe themselves nearly out of existence ("Mum, are you drunk!?!") and pretty much everyone within earshot is in hysterics. She attempts to save face – "Well maybe they have them here... do they? We saw some in Vancouver..." – but the undeniable fact that we are on a lake, rather than the open ocean, means that her voice soon trails off and she prays that no one nearby is writing a travel book and planning on recording the morning for posterity.

We keep an eye out for Orcas as we head out of town to pick up our rental car, our whale spotting hampered by a thickening mist. Breaking through the weather as we drive up through the Crown Pass, we reach the plateau to find Queenstown sheathed in gloom behind us while Wanaka beckons us with UV rays in front. A battle between the sun and looming cloud over Lake Wanaka makes for a suitably biblical backdrop for our lunch, as well as for the famous 'Wanaka Tree'. This is a strange testament to the age of Instagram hype, a willow rising in isolation from just beyond the shores of the lake in a manner sure to make any amateur photographer go weak at the knees. Added to its close proximity to the town centre, as well as a backdrop of snow-tipped mountains just across the water, and you have the perfect storm for a small army of babbling, selfie-snapping tourists. This somewhat takes away from the tree's undoubted aesthetic appeal, especially with a few of the firing squad traversing a small spit of land to have their photo taken next to the unassuming willow, and a quick internet search finds that stories abound of branches actually being damaged by braindead tourists attempting to climb its limbs. Although signs have now been erected around the attraction warning visitors not to attempt this, the idiocy of humankind should never be underestimated and I would be saddened but not surprised to hear of the Wanaka Tree becoming a victim to the relentless pursuit of social media likes.

Five minutes down the road lies an attraction less popular with the tourists, but just as uniquely stunning to my eyes – Wanaka Bowl is an absolute beast of a clover, built next to the old park which has seen better days and quickly becoming home to what seems like a solid scene of next generation transition rippers. The pool coping is perfect, the six foot shallow end consists of one mellow and one whippy pocket, while the deep offers the thrill seeker a fairly hefty ten foot transition topped off with a foot and a half of vert. A few minutes of conversation with the locals soon establishes mutual connections via previous visitors and skate trips past. My brain is filled with the sheer scale of skateboarding's diaspora, picturing global ebbs and flows of stoke, a huge web of restless nomads, the globe criss-crossed with the paths taken by us all in the endless search for what we sensed on some level the first moment we ever stepped out of the front door with a skateboard in hand and even though I am thousands of miles from where I was born I am still home.

The endorphin high carries me through the drizzle-soaked Queenstown evening and is only dampened by a 7am wake up from a drunk American backpacker loudly telling her companions how much she hates the Kardashians. Tourism might be the source of Queenstown's wealth, but I can understand how, for more than one former local we meet further down the line, it is also what drove them to move elsewhere.

Of course, as part of the problem ourselves, we use the early start as an excuse to get on the road, start down Lake Wakatipu and make our way towards the much-lauded tourist destination of Milford Sound. Everyone we have spoken to about our trip has made it very clear that, if we don't pay a visit to Milford Sound, we might as well not bother going at all. The views as we drive down the shore of Lake Wakatipu, captivating to begin with, are slowly replaced by an all-encompassing grey as the cloud sinks inexorably lower. By the time we reach Southland it has cloaked our surroundings in an impenetrable veil and Te Anau is sodden by the time we enter the town, but this should be no surprise for an area known as one of the wettest places on earth, with over 200 days of rainfall annually. We head straight for the nearest book store and I pick up a copy of *Once Were Warriors*, blissfully unaware of the emotional onslaught I am in for. The town is known as the gateway to Fiordland National Park and Milford Sound, but relentless rain and ground-hugging cloud obscures many of the town's unique features and, walking along the banks of Lake Te Anau, the existence of the Murchison Mountain range climbing from the opposing shore is purely academic.

Luckily the elusive takahe is not fussed by a bit of weather, so our visit to the bird sanctuary does not disappoint. New Zealand is rightly famed for its unique, often flightless, often endangered birds, and we aren't one to pass up such an illustrious resident right on our doorstep. Presumed extinct at the end of the 19th century, this stocky, flightless bird bears more than a passing resemblance to its reptilian ancestors. Rediscovered by Dr. Geoffrey Orbell in 1948, in a small enclave deep in the mountains currently obscured from our view by a veil of precipitation, numbers originally decimated by the introduction of stoats and rats by European settlers are beginning to rise in response to a large scale recovery programme. These pests are a massive issue for more than just the takahe and, the closer we get to the sanctuary, the more prevalent the metal boxes at the bases of trees which trap invasive species.

The takahes themselves are in a large enclosure, wandering around aimlessly as if vaguely perturbed by the situation in which they have found themselves. They are an unusual looking bird and, as descriptions go, I probably couldn't do better than the words of a boat crew in the early 20th century which I later find in a *New Zealand Geographic* feature on the bird; "... the size of a goose, with blue-green feathers and the speed of a racehorse." We don't witness much in the way of speed, however; indeed in this weather they are rather sedentary, as are the only other three visitors to the space. It is a hushed, studious environment in which to examine not only these birds – which came so close to extinction – but also the similarly endangered Kākā, the melodious Tui and other native New Zealand bird life. While I can't recommend visiting the sanctuary enough if you find yourself in the town, we are now soaked through and so take refuge in a quiet pub; quiet, at least, until a group of elderly, tipsy Americans walk in at the same time that a rugby game featuring Team USA starts on the TV. The scene quickly descends into a nightmare of national anthem singin', USA-rootin', hand on heart Frankenstein's Monster made up of organised sports and nationalism, so we beat a hasty retreat back to our holiday park and a more palatable drinking environment.

The early exit from the pub is not necessarily a bad thing, as our tour out to Milford Sound takes off from Te Anau early the next morning. We set off in the tour bus, a full house of couples and families all studiously avoiding eye contact with each other, while our driver and guide gives us a spiel on the surrounding countryside and what weather we can expect for the day. The farmland which surrounds Te Anau gradually gives way to rugged foothills and we realise what a difference the change in conditions will make as, against all odds, it looks as if we'll be able to see further than two feet in front of us by the time we reach the Sound itself. The rain recedes at pace with signs of human habitation as the sheer overwhelming order of agriculture is replaced by an altogether more chaotic backdrop, a monument to the raw power of nature.

The sun is glinting off the snow capped peaks of The Divide and distant waterfalls crashing down the rock face with the force of a thousand herds of bull elephants are reduced to gentle trickles by the enormity of the landscape of which they are a part. It is a forbidding sight, a world of hidden caves never seen by the eyes of man, of subzero temperatures and sudden avalanches, of Lovecraftian myth and the barely realised terror of our own microscopic size in a universe of unspeakable proportion. Yet it is one still teeming with life. It would have been even further into the inhospitable depths of this ancient seismic upheaval that the last of the takahe were found, and this is still home to many species which have become scarce in other parts of the country.

It is before the Homer Tunnel crossing when we get our first sighting of the kea – the 'clown of the mountains' – a highly intelligent branch of the parrot genus infamous for their inquisitive nature and lack of shyness. Notorious for the damage they can inflict on tourist's cars, with a particular taste for hooking their beaks into the rubber seals which ring door frames, curiosity has also killed the kea on more than one occasion – breaking into the aforementioned pest boxes only to find them tightly packed with angry, hungry stoats. Local conservation groups are on the third attempt at designing a Kea-proof box, which they are hoping will finally prove successful. With thankfully no predator-filled pest boxes nearby at the moment, the bird here is happy playing to an audience; ripping at car antennas, intimidating two German girls trying to get back into their car and putting one small boy on our tour group into full flight with a sudden spread of its wings and ungainly run at the unfortunate child.

With some more rare wildlife sightings under our belt, we carry on through the Homer Tunnel, a 1.2km hole hewn through the granite of the Darran Ranges. It is an engineering feat made all the more impressive by the fact that, when work on the tunnel first began in 1935, it was by a mere five men with pickaxes and presumably little aversion to cold weather. It wasn't completed until 1954, and has since facilitated tourist entry to what has been dubbed the eighth natural wonder of the world. The camp in which these hardy workers lived during the build, battling arctic conditions and minimal amenities, was pitched on Knobs Flat – a fact now celebrated with the annual Homer Tunnel Nude Run, which takes place at the beginning of winter and sounds in no way tempting, despite being described by one local as "invigorating, natural and beautiful". It isn't in fact entirely naked – participants are granted the luxury of running shoes and a headlamp – but, having been through fully clothed and in a vehicle, I can't say I'm in a rush to get back to experience it as nature intended.

The sight which greets you as you exit the tunnel on the Milford Sound side, however, will have all thoughts of blue-tinged genitalia banished from your mind. The road hits the open air and suddenly starts swerving as if its builders had been dodging bullets, at the same time beginning a vertiginous descent through the Cleddau Valley towards the Sound itself. These hairpin turns offer a range of awe-inspiring snapshots of the peaks which loom above the valley, occasionally darting off into clearings which act as the starting point for the numerous mountain treks, or 'tramps', available through the region. These range from straightforward half-hour strolls to serious five day hikes, depending on your level of hardiness, but with snow still on the peaks and avalanche season only just past we opt out of any serious tramps. By the time our bus reaches the water and we climb aboard the ferry for the waterbound part of our tour, we should rightly be jaded to natural wonder; but Milford Sound just keeps ramping up the natural splendour, with sun dappled water fed by falls streaming from the surrounding cliff faces all the way out to the Tasman Sea. Colonies of seals sun themselves on the rocks, improbable vegetation clings to sheer rock, the universe narrows itself down to this point, this moment, this scene in front of us and everything else is merely a grey dream, a pimple waiting to be burst on the face of whatever higher being created this wondrous landscape. We return to Te Anau in the unique situation of being genuinely exhausted by beauty.

With this in mind, we could never expect too much from the attractions to be found between Te Anau and Dunedin; the Milton Kink, however, manages to underwhelm even our low expectations. The majority of New Zealand travel websites have placed this one high in their lists of tourist attractions in the area; a stretch of asphalt which suddenly and without warning zags a full road's width sideways, it is the small town of Milton's one claim to fame and has obviously been such a boon to local tourism that, as you enter the outskirts of Milton coming from Te Anau, you will encounter 'The Kink in the Road Cafe'. In fact it is so arresting that, driving through the town in another thick downpour, we don't even realise that we have navigated the kink until we are clear of the town and deduce that we must have done so. Thankfully, Dunedin makes up in droves what the preceding drive may lack. A city well built for the weather which has followed us from Te Anau, it is a warren of hillside haunts and low lit bars, museums and bookstores and mists parting to reveal tantalising glimpses of the bay before again descending. Central to the city's indoor attractions is the Otago Museum, home to the only Moai Statue in New Zealand and paean to species passed into the history books. You can't move in New Zealand without bumping into information on a species which just couldn't adapt to the ascension of mankind, whether hunted for food to extinction or wiped out by animals introduced from Europe or the South Pacific. Most impressive amongst these is the flightless Moa, a bird which stood well over the height of a man and of which you can find skeletons at various museums across the two islands. The various species of Moa and the similarly huge Haast's Eagle (with a wingspan of 3 metres) are the most iconic faces of Aotearoa extinction, but the list is extensive; the adzebill, the south island snipe, the laughing owl, bell wren, huia, New Zealand quail, New Zealand musk duck, and many more. As these are only the ones known to modern science, it is no stretch to imagine this as the tip of an iceberg forever lost to us. It is a common story, but somehow the tragedy seems much more immediate here; perhaps due to the primordial surroundings in which we have spent the last few days, perhaps because some of the creatures now past were being seen well into the 20th century, perhaps because birds like the takahe, kea and kiwi are so close to joining this tragic list.

Dry weather is a distant memory and small streams trickle through the streets and make a thick paste of thousands of fake banknotes strewn beneath our feet as we run between bars.

"MONEY CAN BUY HAPPINESS", states the top line of text printed on these, followed with "But no amount of money can save you from the grave." This cheery tract offers advice on how to avoid eternal damnation, including daily bible readings and handy prayers which offer a repenting of sins, but apparently forgot the bit about not fucking littering. These droppings add a gaudy tone to Dunedin's pavement as well as an air of rambling insanity to its social milieu, which thankfully is of a much more sensible, secular air within its pubs. Whilst smaller cities might lack the array of nightlife that London or Melbourne can boast, in places like Dunedin a modest CBD (Central Boozing District) is used to the punter's and the business' advantage and pretty much every place which pours a pint is full of people drinking, dancing and laughing. For two nights we reel through the city streets, the drizzle framed by street lights soaking our clothes and leaving us bedraggled as we befriend bartenders and sample the fruits of New Zealand's thriving independent beer industry. Despite the inclement two day hangover, when the rain finally thins on our last day in town I'm not going to miss the opportunity to skate the infamous Blood Bucket, looming large in New Zealand skate-lore from its position in the hills of Mornington. Originally built in 1981, due to the slow trickle of skate media to New Zealand at the time the bowl is modelled on 1970s designs and has no flat bottom, a concrete lip and a roll in which in no way assists in figuring out the lines. Luckily I have local legend Morph to show me how it should be skated, but even so I feel like I'd need a month of sessions to skate it how I'd like to. That isn't to say fun isn't had – half the joy of these ancient concrete obscurities is figuring out how to claw speed from a strange corner, a harsh kink or a sloping, mellow transition. The hillbomb back into Dunedin is the icing on the cake, even if it shaves a couple of millimetres off of my wheels.

The landscape begins to flatten itself out as you drive north of the city and the usual internet sources aren't offering much in the way of sightseeing between now and Timaru – not even another kink in the road to marvel over – but a snap decision to follow a brown road sign finds us at the brilliant Moeraki Boulders. A natural phenomenon caused by erosion of nearby cliffs, these spherical rocks lie like discarded marbles of the gods over a stretch of Koekohe Beach, a strange corner of Aotearoa terra firma which we have nearly to ourselves. Of varying sizes, with the largest over two metres in width, they range in appearance from perfect ovals to cracked shapes resembling the fossilized remains of an egg belonging to some creature even larger than the moa. There's one which even looks like the Wu-Tang Clan's logo, if you squint hard enough. Similarly strange is the next town on the map's claim to fame. Oamaru is 'New Zealand's steampunk capital' – a point emphasised at both ends of the town by giant sculptures stating the fact – and, if I had any kind of journalistic curiosity I would have stopped in the town, spoken to a few locals and at least gained a few anecdotes about how this small farming community became a lightning rod for such an obscure subculture. However, you've unfortunately been reading a book written by someone who thinks goggles and old dresses are shite, so we drive straight through to Timaru and head down to what turns to be an absolute death trap of a skatepark. The amount of obstacles which lead directly into walls or sharply angled concrete means that after ten minutes I decide to quit while I'm ahead, though a surprisingly well made bank to wall keeps me entertained for that brief period. Weirdly enough it appears briefly on Anti Hero's New Zealand tour video *A Body Corporate* (Grant Taylor flying out of a quarter to frontside truck bash on the bank to wall), and what they made of the park I can only guess at – however, later in the week a Christchurch local tells me that a few years ago the local council somehow managed to schedule a demo from none other than Tony Hawk. Not long before the event in question, photos of the park reached the Birdman and the demo was immediately cancelled. Considering the injury which was soon to befall me, this reticence to skate seems amusing; but hindsight is essentially a bastard, and for now we head to the bar safe in the knowledge that we've dodged both slams and people who think monocles are cool.

Christchurch, our destination the next morning, is a city still very much on a path to recovery. A number of major earthquakes hit the city between 2010 and 2012, with the second earthquake on the 22nd of February 2011 causing 185 deaths. The combined force of the other quakes took a heavy toll on the city's architecture and the CBD seen from above would appear as if nestled in the centre of a giant building site. At the centre of this can be found 185 white chairs; a commemoration to those lost to the earthquake arranged by local artist Peter Majendie. It stands, along with the crumbling remains of the old cathedral, as a stark and truly touching tribute. Within a few blocks of both of these can be found both the official memorial and 'Quake City', an earthquake centre detailing the disaster. It is a sunny, pleasant day when we arrive in the city, the main streets are filled with a relaxed crowd of both tourists and locals and it is hard to imagine just how terrifying it must have been to be here when the earth turned itself inside out; but, in the midst of its rise from the ashes, Christchurch is a city determined not to forget those it lost. It is also a city sprinkled with numerous social initiatives to draw people back to the city, including the awe inspiring Washington Way Skatepark (more of which to come).

Sometimes it seems like a giant playground, one in which we play giant Space Invaders projected onto the walls of buildings, drink cheap Pacific malt liquor and wander through sculpture exhibitions taking up entire city blocks as we catch up with friends. Garry and Sarah were in the city during the 2019 attacks and took shelter in the Christchurch Library, a huge building with myriad free facilities ranging from a recording studio to 3D printers. It is clearly one of their favourite aspects of Christchurch and I can see why – if more urban centres had libraries so accessible and with so many things to offer, it could only be of benefit to society. I will not credit the perpetrator of the 2019 terrorist atrocities in Christchurch by using his name, but coming as it did in the midst of what seems to be such a positive regeneration it is especially tragic. The city we find is one of friendship and respect, in which a wide array of cultures have come together in resolve to rebuild. The religious and racial divides upon which he based his ideologies are ones of a twisted evil mind, but unfortunately part of a wider spectrum of right wing populism across the globe. With the mainstream media often playing up issues and spreading divisiveness between communities, seeing the people of Christchurch coming together to try and solve their issues and make sure something like this can never happen again is truly heartening.

Washington Way Skatepark is a microcosm of this positivity, a place which I am drawn back to time and time again which offers up the cross section of humanity you can find at any major skate scene hub. Built in 2014, it is a massive 3.2million dollar concrete playground which has almost everything you could want from a skatepark. A bowl with a cradle and a deep end designed to appease the most jaded of old vert skaters, an extensive street course, a smaller flow bowl and a variety of transitions of varying steepness, the park has clearly fired up the local scene in a way that only a few select skateparks can. A community's cohesiveness is often no stronger than at the local skatepark or street spot and Christchurch's skateboarders and BMXers are clearly a tight knit group. On my last visit, I get talking to an older skater who introduces himself with "They call me 'Gnarly'". He is homeless, a Dunedin resident escaping the winter down south in Christchurch's more temperate climes. Currently living under the bridge just around the corner from the park, he clearly channels the full force of long term frustration at the cards dealt by life, the true grim permanence of social immobility, into his frontside grinds. Upon hearing that I have visited the Blood Bucket, he bemoans the fall off in the scene down that way; "Supposedly skating has progressed, but I don't see kids doing what those guys were doing there at that time." This is not an accusation that can be levelled at the skaters of Christchurch, who clearly know their way around the big bowl. They are full of an energy which I can see pervading the whole city. Dunedin I love for it settledness, its deep roots by the bay and sense of being a place of social gathering for millennia past; Christchurch, I love for its seeming constant momentum. It is as if some of the tectonic force which resides deep in the ground below, that which has been such a scourge to the city's inhabitants, has in some way been harnessed and channelled into a vibrant cultural milieu. It is a city for which things are undoubtedly looking up.

Over our travels thus far, more than one person has laid down convincing arguments for us to travel up the West Coast. "The East is dull", they say, "It's just farmland, grass and sheep; you want the real New Zealand, head for the mountains in the West." A quick look at the forecast on either side convinces us to go against popular opinion and stick with the sheep, grass and most importantly sunshine. Doing away with our hire car and catching a bus up to Kaikoura, it immediately becomes clear that, for those who were so dismissive of this area, familiarity has bred an uncalled-for contempt. I worry for a second that it is no different from all those times I've slated East Sussex, but then consider Eastbourne – and all issues relating to – and decide that no, I am right to judge. Eastbourne is faded Victorian grandeur seen through a lens of smack addiction, blinding arcade machine lights and pitbull-sized seagulls. Kaikoura is a town elegantly caught between sea and mountain range, peppered on its coastal side by jagged rocks poking from the water like the teeth of some fallen leviathan. We strain our eyes in the twilight gloom trying to spot whales, before giving up and retreating to the town's welcoming drinking establishments. It turns out that whales are best seen from the various boats which operate out of the town and, as our budget is fairly tight, we abandon the hunt for ocean-going mammals and carry on up the island via public transport.

Buses over here are much more palatable than the special circle of hell that is the Megabus (or its polished turd of a cousin, National Express), in no small part due to their drivers – a tribe of eccentric, white haired old Kiwis armed with an arsenal of tidbits about their routes ranging from the informative to the strangely personal; "Here there used to be a cheese factory, but it burned down...which wasn't very good...because it was very nice cheese." We are now in wine country, the sunniest part of an island otherwise famed for its precipitation, and far from being the preserve of bus drivers eccentricity is worn as a badge of honour. This is epitomised by the middle-aged American woman who greets us at the Atlantis Backpackers hotel, paint in her hair and a cat on the countertop nuzzling against her face as she finds our booking. She is larger than life, a frustrated thespian who lectures on jazz over breakfast and takes in stray cats, gushes over a musician's recent visit and manages to fit the term 'boogie woogie' into conversation more than anyone I've ever met, or expect to meet. These quirks extend to the area's skateparks too, from Picton's 8ft concrete midiramp with a metal angle iron for coping, to Nelson and its Gulliver's kidney bowl; features which somehow don't detract from the builds, rather adding a haphazard charm to what would otherwise be monotonously uniform council-built skateparks.

Nelson also has a geographical claim to fame, positioned as it is in the dead centre of New Zealand. I'm standing in the kitchen of our backpackers, trying desperately to deflect a determined football fan from talking about Chelsea. He has assumed that as a Brit I must love the sport, and even an attempt to dead end the conversation with the unsubtle "I know nothing about it and it doesn't interest me" falls flat, so in desperation I cut in and ask about local walks. When he responds with "Well you could walk to the centre of New Zealand," I assume that it's the beginning of a strange sports joke, but upon further research it is established that the geographical centre of the country is indeed only a half hour walk from where we stand. I extricate myself from a second bout of football appreciation ("When they ask for my religion on job application sheets, I need a box for soccer"), we grab some cans and head up the steep hillside path to find not only panoramic views of the surrounding area but also a small plaque placing the spot with a giant steel pencil suspended above it; adding a serendipitously literary feel to our booze-fuelled human bullseye.

CHAPTER TWELVE

Liver damage and cerebral bruising

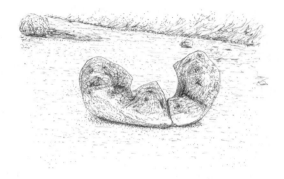

Heading back to Picton the next day, we hop on the ferry to Wellington and find ourselves sat between a pleasantly stereotypical grey nomad couple from the US and a weathered Dutch woman nursing a glass of white wine in the corner and enjoying a break from the weather currently lashing her home on the west coast. They keep pointing out landmarks and taking punts on what they might be, she keeps correcting them. They are clearly irritating one another no end, so to avoid getting embroiled we head to the deck to finish our drinks and continue our ultimately unsuccessful quest to see whales and albatrosses. The west coast weather is thankfully localised and the journey between the islands is calm and uneventful, although you wouldn't think it looking at some of the more seasickness-prone passengers. They have yet to realise that the mental disequilibrium caused by alcohol is actually key to offsetting the nausea which a gently swaying ferry can bring on, and for this lack of knowledge they are clearly suffering. Similar, but much scarier, levels of movement can be found on the rickety wooden structures which offer precarious parking on the steeper regions of the nation's capital. Wellington is a city clinging onto its surrounding hills for dear life, something no more noticeable than when these structures appear amongst the hairpin turns which wind up amongst sheer walls and imposing colonial buildings. I'm sure that they must be safe, as the residents seem to take them as a given and there were no news reports of anyone being crushed by falling cars while we were there, but for the uninitiated they are a subtly, almost subconsciously anxiety-inducing sight.

Keeping a careful eye on the hills above us, we pay a visit the next morning to the city's extensive Botanic Gardens. Originally conceived as a more formal layout, in recent years native bush has been allowed and indeed actively encouraged to reclaim a huge space right in the centre of the city. While the rose gardens and sculpture parks are there for those who want them, it is the areas which suddenly find you cut off from both the city and the hand of man which stand out. The native tui, their complex calls the result of having two voice boxes, flit through the branches; offering a melodious and varied soundtrack to the tumultuous greens and browns of Aoteroa's flora, so different from the manicured formality envisaged by those homesick European settlers who began the project in 1844. At the bottom of the gardens greenery is supplanted by concrete and the city centre spreads all the way down to the waterfront, surrounded by lush green hills and offering plenty in the way of museums, cafes and bars. Wellington's skate scene turns out to be one of the best I come across during my travels, although I get off to an inauspicious start when I arrive at the legendary Waitangi Park bowl to find it in the midst of being painted. Three skaters sitting by the shallow end debating a Plan B give me a combination of friendly nod and helpless shrug before heading out, upon which I instigate my own back-up plan. Before leaving Melbourne I had been in touch with Flynn, a Brit transplant who is heavily involved with the local DIY build. With a location saved in my phone and the promise of a session later in the day once people got out of work, I grab a six-pack and head up there to get a head start. The Ghetto Spot is an ode to gnarly, steep transition, with the one mellow quarter toughened up by Salba Sauce-free exposed aggregate coping. Broken glass and gravel crunches under urethane relentlessly, spilling blood is a given and it is safe to say that the crew here are carving their own unique slice of hostile Gnartopia. All possible props to those getting out there and building the obstacles they want to skate, rather than waiting on the hand of Babylon to feed them.

The beautiful ugliness inherent in DIY skate spots is mirrored in Ronnie Van Hout's 'Quasi', an eye catching sculpture of a sentient hand poised above the City Gallery. When first unveiled in Christchurch it provoked mixed reactions, with one local art critic starting a petition calling for its banishment from the city. This is all the incentive me and Alyce need to head inside while we wait for a double tattoo appointment but, while it is novelty that draws us in, it is the 'Eavesdropping' exhibition that captivates us. Showcasing the work of a number of artists and activists surrounding issues of hearing and listening in an increasingly digital age, with all the inherent discussions around state and corporate surveillance this raises, it covers subjects ranging from Somalians being denied refugee status on the basis of accent tests to redacted accounts of the Watergate Scandal. One piece focuses on the idea of a 'panacousticon', an aural Panopticon* developed in the 1600s in which courtiers could eavesdrop on the proletariat via giant funnels hidden within walls. An illustration from the time, demonstrating the apparatus and amusing on first inspection, quickly loses its novelty when the underlying idea is applied to monitoring of social media and search engine use; in essence, we have been duped into creating our own funnels. At a time when Big Brother can be assumed to almost always be watching, acts such as the DIY build just up the road are one of the many ways in which we can reclaim our sense of freedom and, by proxy, our own identity.

Paranoia well and truly activated, we head out of the City Gallery and towards The Gallery Tattoo Studio to distract ourselves from the increasingly Orwellian cast of Western society with an ode to one of my favourite films.

* Theoretical prison designed in the 18th century by Jeremy Bentham in which the entire prison could be controlled by a single guard due to the prisoners having no idea as to when they were being watched.

Wandering around Wellington, I've found it impossible to not have scenes from *Braindead* playing on repeat just below the surface of my consciousness. Peter Jackson's third feature-length film, using Wellington as its backdrop, is high in the 80s horror pantheon. While I don't have much time for touring filming locations during our visit (I'd take the Porirua Pinnacles over Hobbiton any day if I did), I do make an appointment to see Yorkshire pal Jord, who is working for a tattoo studio and is more than happy to give me a permanent memento of the city in the form of the film's zombifying instigator, the Sumatran Rat Monkey. While I had no plans on skating so soon after getting tattooed, due to the inherent danger of slamming on a part of my body recently stabbed repeatedly with a tiny needle, Wellington bowl is now invitingly free of wet paint. I decide to make the most of the post-ink adrenaline rush and get stuck in once I've swept out the drifts of broken glass presumably left by the previous day's artists/disrespectful wankers. I'm glad that I do, because this turns out to be one of the best bowls of Aotearoa – deep, whippy, lumpy and with coping that barks like a rabid hyena when you lock into a grind. My skate urges are satisfied by the time Alyce's (non-Braindead themed) tattoo is finished, so we head to a pub which happens to be serving $5 pints on a Wednesday, cementing Wellington's place as one of my favourite cities on earth.

We are, however, on a tight schedule, so – after a morning educating ourselves on natural history in the incredible Te Papa Museum and fitting in one last roll around the bowl – we find ourselves that afternoon driving out into Martinborough, the North Island's wine country. Featherstone, one of the many small, well-off country towns dotted around the region, is our base and an ideal launching point for visiting multiple purveyors of grape-based boozing. The area is clearly well-off, wine has been a boon industry and the abundance of posh cafes and adverts for high tea speak of middle class affluence, but an undercurrent of rural life still gleams through via the dry-skinned drinkers in the back street RSLs and the speed with which suburbia succumbs to bushland and paddocks. The stark sight of cars swerving a deer head and hooves gathering flies on the main street as we walk out looking for breakfast one morning is presumably related in some way to farming and hunting rather than Satanic rituals gone awry, but I don't know that for sure. Resisting the temptation of a roadkill fry-up to start the day, we grab pastries and head down to Cape Palliser. This unsung gem of the New Zealand countryside is found at the end of a winding, barely maintained country road which is being gradually eaten away by the ocean. After a few slow zig zags around chunks of road reclaimed by Poseidon (not the one we stayed with on the Gold Coast), we park up next to a colony of especially fragrant seals and stroll up to the lighthouse. It is an area which runs adjacent to the Porirua Pinnacles (or 'Skull Island', the location of the opening scene to Braindead), so the geography gives the film nerd in me great pleasure and even without the lure of Rat Monkeys it is still an arresting sight; a diorama of serrated rock sawing at cerulean skies, its harshness softened by the deep green grass which brightens the countryside from coast to coast on both islands. We head on to Masterton, buoyed by the scenery around us, to the B'n' B we have booked for the night. As we pull up in the driveway, a brittley posh middle aged woman runs out to show us how the house's various amenities work. Pointing at the TV, she admits it doesn't work too well before killing any chance of civility with the statement "We can blame the Asians for that." After a few more similar attempts at the Jim Davidson school of humour, alongside a particularly backwards monologue on "the problems with Maoris up north" and her issues with the amount of funding their communities received, it was clear that her and her husband (quietly supportive of her distasteful spiel) were bigoted morons. Perhaps their minds were rotted away from the trappings of wealth and the proximity of all that cheap wine, perhaps they were wankers to begin with, but either way we make our viewpoints just as clear and retreat from conversation at the earliest opportunity.

Some days, you wake up with an impending feeling of doom. You look three or four times each way before crossing the road, avoid walking under ladders, stay back from cliff edges and try as hard as you can to hunker down and let whatever dark cloud your subconscious has picked up on pass by. These are not the days that you will get fucked up; when the universe wants to slap you down, it will sneak up on you like a thief in the night.

We hit the road early the next morning, meeting up with some friends and enjoying company that doesn't involve casual racism. Lucy is the head of a project which focuses on intergenerational connections and fosters a feeling of community, with the conversation a world away from the small minded vitriol of our previous night's hosts. Hitting the road for Palmerston North we have a renewed feeling of optimism, the kind that the discussion of personal projects with truly driven individuals can induce, and once we arrive I decide to take a look at the local skatepark.

How it was, I couldn't really tell you. I recall a couple of runs working out some strange kinks, a waterfall with a lip and a few odd lumps in the transition. Then suddenly everything is eclipsed by explosions of red fireworks; intricate phosphenes blooming like supernovae before fading away to reveal snatches of past, present and future, complete clarity and utter confusion arm-in-arm like scheming lovers, photo images cascading like tetris blocks before fading into the depths unordered, the atom and the milky way, angels fucking on the head of a pin and then I wake up in an ambulance covered in blood and suffering from a heavy concussion. It takes twelve staples to pin down the flap of skin on my head and I still have no idea exactly how I slammed; in fact, it takes a couple of hours in the hospital before my scrambled brain can even put together the events of the day leading up to the skate. I don't remember the skateboarders who peeled me off of the flat bottom, but much love to them, the paramedics who drove me to hospital and the doctors and nurses who stapled my head back together and didn't once ask me if I was too old to be doing this. One day when I find myself back in Palmerston North, it's my round. In the meantime, with driving nixed for the day due to my ongoing concussion, we wander along the riverbank, consume some probably ill-advised adult beverages and ponder a line from Henry Miller's *The Colossus of Maroussi*; "I was never more certain that life and death were one and that neither can be enjoyed or embraced if the other be absent."

My injury puts our tightly packed schedule a little off kilter, but I wake up feeling oddly refreshed by the combination of cerebral bruising and liver abuse and thoroughly enjoy the drive to Taupo along the Desert Road. A stretch of tarmac connecting two ends of a volcanic plateau, it is at once desolate – more redolent of *Mad Max* than anything I have driven across in New Zealand or even Australia – and dotted with snapshot moments of nature's brilliance framed by arid wasteland.

We stop for lunch at what seems at first glance to be one of these oases, but the wads of toilet paper rolling lazily across the floor and clinging to low hanging branches by the water are a clear warning to tread carefully. Who knows, maybe trucker shit is by some strange twist of fate nature's perfect fertiliser, something to do with the way methamphetamines break down the trans fats in McDonald's meals? Perhaps this is the root cause of the proliferation of greenery which bursts forth from the dust surrounding us, but either way I don't want to spend the afternoon picking it out of my waffle grip. The wheels keep turning, past army bases and prison camps, animal carcasses and carrion birds tugging stringy lumps of flesh from bone. Benighted shrubs dot a landscape ringed in the near distance by mountains thrusting from the earth like sentinels guarding some half forgotten world of gods and monsters and blood and fire. It is a scene of bleak, violent beauty, one which does not invite the human spirit to contemplate habitation.

Thus our arrival at the green and scenic town of Taupo, on the shore of the lake of the same name, offers up a strange mental dislocation; passing through such varied landscapes in such a short amount of time is one of New Zealand's more discombobulating charms. Not as charming is the smug racism which we again experience at a pub that evening, from yet another odious xenophobe who assumes that, as we're white, we must want to be taken into confidence with sneering attacks on the local Maori community. As we have stopped in the town specifically to see the large Maori carvings on the lake, this behaviour is even more of a shock than it was coming from an elderly couple in a predominantly white, middle class town. Many Australians I speak to have described New Zealand wistfully as more forward thinking than their own, but it seems as if attitudes still have a way to go before this can become a reality.

The next morning, we head out to see the carvings under the care of an alarmingly cavalier captain, who seemingly isn't fussed about either the high winds raking up a chop on the lake or letting his charges know that they should attach bags firmly to something nailed down – in fact it is a fellow passenger who tells us that we are about to lose our meagre possessions to the deep, as we grip the railing with white knuckles and the surface of the water gets closer to our faces with every turn of the boat. We are crammed in a corner too far from the front to hear the highlights of our captain's tour spiel, but it is clear that handing out crackers to feed the ducks flying alongside the boat (obviously used to this free feed) is what he is here for. He guides us at full speed through the swells, the boat lurching from port to starboard as we careen around the headland, before finally coming to rest by the carvings; a huge tattooed face cut from the raw cliff face by Maori carver Matahi Whakataka-Brightwell, who began creating this imposing work in 1976 and completed it over the course of four years. A 14 metre high likeness of an ancestral Maori figure, it dominates Mine Bay with a gravitas which belies its relatively recent origins; seeming more a recently rediscovered historical wonder.

Ngatoroirangi was a Maori navigator who guided the Tuwharetoa and Te Arawa tribes to the area over a thousand years ago. The irony of our captain only being able to guide us to the carvings for about twenty seconds, before he takes us back into a rollercoaster of heavy swells and well-fed ducks, is not lost upon us. Reaching dry land wobbly-legged, not much the wiser, but thankfully still in possession of our bags, we go for a walk through the gorge and are quickly immersed in the bushland which crowds the bank of the Waikato River. The gorge is popular with adrenaline junkies, offering bungee jumps and cliff swings, but I'm happy getting my kicks from nearly dying in concrete holes in the ground so we stick to the various walks which the area has to offer.

The next day we head to one such concrete hole which stands tall in New Zealand skate lore. Melville Bowl sits potent and foreboding on the outskirts of Hamilton, imbued with the weight of generations of ripping. I'm under doctor's orders to not partake in anything which may result in further cranial trauma for another three weeks, so it's really a stroke of luck for my gray matter that the park is in the middle of a full refurb and not skateable. The site workers are nice enough to give me a tour of the resurfaced bowl and the outline of what will by the looks of things be a huge street course. As positive as it is to see money being put into these projects by councils, a part of me is saddened by seeing some of the bowl's unique charms smoothed out by fresh concrete and brand new coping. It is the imperfections, the harshness, the innate gnarliness of weathered concrete dinosaurs which has drawn Cardiel, Beres, Raemers and so many more to spots like this over the years. Melbourne has had multiple new parks built in the last couple of years, but I still have more fun skating Dorfus' designs in Epping and Point Cook, or Coburg's whiplash-inducing kidney bowl, or Corio's crumbling edifices.

If you want your faith restored in the survival of Jurassic concrete, however, Auckland is the place to be. Plunging into the city's tangled road network, we somehow manage to navigate some of its more confusing turns and reach New Lynn Skatepark without too much fuss. I've managed three days since the knockout without skating and it seems fitting that the first park I skate post-head injury is one that was clearly designed by someone with a head injury. Built in the 1970s or 80s, although no one I speak to can actually pin down a date, the story goes that the builders took the plans, the measurements of which were laid out in Imperial, and accidentally designed the place in Metric. The result is a park not suitable for those prone to claustrophobia or tight trucks, but still offers up way more fun than the yawnfest that is Victoria Park skatepark in Auckland's CBD. Featuring a lesson in how not to build a bowl – mellow, kinked curves and too much flat – it also offers a variety of crumbling ledges, a rotting miniramp and a giant transitioned flatbank which Ben Raemers backside bonelessed for a Volcom edit many moons ago. This was skate stopped when a local died attempting to drop in, with the council's hastily erected barbed wire along the lip more reminiscent of prison guard tower than skatepark obstacle. In my mind I'm transported to the series of *The Walking Dead* set in an abandoned prison, desperately attempting to ward off the scooter hordes tailwhipping viciously at our ankles. My low tolerance this day for both badly-poured concrete and the scooting dead probably has something to do with the $6 bottles of beer, being sold cheap to make way for new stock, that we consumed the previous night; drinking in New Zealand definitely doesn't have the same hassle attached to it as it does in Australia, especially when it comes to your wallet. Therefore, while Victoria Park isn't the best park I've skated in the last few weeks by a long shot, it does fulfill the vital task of letting me sweat my hangover out before heading to Lynfield – an Auckland skatepark nearly as iconic as New Lynn. With a small but fast snake run and a whippy hourglass bowl which demands a fairly high level of attention to navigate without losing a few teeth, this one can be seen at various points throughout Anti Hero's New Zealand tour video *A Body Corporate* being shredded in a manner which, having now been there, I can safely describe as 'unlikely'. I stay there for some time. I skate in turns by myself, or with locals ranging in age from early teens to mid-40s. I chat for some time with a family recently emigrated from Northern China, who are astonished at the park's longevity. The lip upon which my trucks are crunching has been feeling the same caress for forty years, from pros and beginners, living legends and those no longer with us, nomadic adrenaline seekers from across the globe. To the uninitiated it may look like nothing more than a middlingly intimidating set of transitions, but though skateboarding may be young its history has quickly flung off temporal constraints and bound in this concrete is a millennia of shared experience. Every session, every time we leave the house on four wheels, every time we roll the dice, in an alternate universe we die a thousand deaths, suffer a thousand injuries; this is what will keep skateboarding ever apart from becoming a mere sport, this is what imbues spots like Lynfield with such gravitas. Standing up on a frontside pivot, a small chunk of concrete is knocked loose and tumbles down the transition. I put it into a pocket of my bag, another memento from the never ending road.

EPILOGUE

We return to Australia to find the East Coast in flames. Bushfires are raging through Queensland and New South Wales, feeding on dry fuel sources which follow on from a record-breaking drought season. Hundreds of homes have been destroyed, lives have been lost and smoke is causing an unprecedented rise in respiratory problems as urban centres are cloaked in thick clouds of smoke. Through the maelstrom strides a familiar figure; totemic head of the coal industry's PR department and crusher of environmental dissidence, Scott Morrison, to laugh in the face of those who connect this natural disaster to man-made issues. He has already begun to lay the groundworks for his continued domination over the rest of the century. The farmers must pray for rain and Australia's consistent wooing of the fossil industry is entirely unrelated to the apocalyptic conditions ravaging the eastern fringe of the country. Whispers of him visiting certain specialised doctors adept in the art of biomechanics are suppressed even quicker than the climate protesters who would hamper the businesses to whom ScoMo is beholden. He has been waiting for this moment, the reckoning of which his religion so keenly awaits, and rest assured he will not be unprepared when the time comes. While millions perish, while the earth itself lashes out in self defence, his titanium frame will render him impervious as he holds up his sacrificial lambs to his uncaring god and ushers in a new era on this dead planet.

The Ben Raemers Foundation

In May 2019, at the age of 28, professional skateboarder Ben Raemers took his own life. His passion for life and skateboarding has always been contagious. Ben will be remembered by all as a loving son, brother, friend and inspiration.

The Ben Raemers Foundation aims to end the stigma and burden that so often clouds issues of mental health by bringing awareness of these issues and suicide to the forefront within the wider skateboarding community.

For more information and how you could support the Foundation please visit:

https://benraemersfoundation.com

THANKS
(Also no thanks)

Alyce, for everything, but specifically in this case for being a top road companion and car journey DJ/Purveyor of Snacks.
The extended Kitching family, for always putting us up and helping us out across NSW and beyond.
Jodie Cooke, whose constructive feedback helped me believe that this project could happen.

Big love to everyone who put us up, sat at the bar with us and helped bring about some of the best skateboarding (and otherwise) adventures of my life;

Queensland:
Dan Stirling and Elisha Spackman, Sarah and Phil, Garry Giomarelli, Manu and Brenno, Jordy Figallo and the Brisbane miniramp house party crew, Erik Cole

New South Wales and Australian Capital Territory:
Nathan, James and the Sydney skate crew, Yogs and Liam

New Zealand:
Luna and Timmy, Morph, Zedyn and family, Flynn Acworth, Axel, Georgia Hudson and the Wellington DIY crew, Jord Nötter, Palmerston North paramedics, nurses and doctors

Melbourne:
Curty, Josh Leishman, Joey Graham, Adam Jeffreson, Dom, Cuzza, Rosie, Luke Johnson, Grizz, Bellamy, Jayden, Tom 'Gorm' Lillingstone, Will Hewitt, Fionn Dempsey, Fitzy crew, Woodies Hotel crew, Hemley Skate Shop, Coburg Kidney Bowl

No thanks:

The person who did a shit in the bowl the day of my leaving do.

BIBLIOGRAPHY

Abbott, E. (1864). 'Slippery Bob' recipe in *The English and Australian Cookery Book: Cooking for the Many, as well as the Upper Ten Thousand*. London: Sampson Low, Son and Marston

Ballard, JG. (1975). *High Rise*. London: Jonathan Cape

Bourdain, A. (2001). *A Cook's Tour: In Search of the Perfect Meal*. New York: Bloomsbury

Burge, M. (2011). 'How the Aboriginal Legend of the Three Sisters Trumped a Tall Story', *Blue Mountains Life Magazine*, December-January 2011. Available at: https://burgewords.com/2013/04/15/the-tale-of-a-legend/

Di Justo, P. (2013). *'The Cicada's Love Affair with Prime Numbers'*, The New Yorker, May 13th 2013. Available at: https://www.newyorker.com/tech/elements/the-cicadas-love-affair-with-prime-numbers

Frei, P. (2011). *Discussion on the Meaning of 'Canberra'*. Available at: https://web.archive.org/web/20130927182307/http://www.canberrahistoryweb.com/meaningofcanberra.htm

Grzelewski, D. (1999). *'Takahe – The Bird That Came Back from the Dead'*, New Zealand Geographic, I ssue 41, Jan-Mar 1999. Available at: https://www.nzgeo.com/stories/takahe-the-bird-that-came-back-from-the-dead/

Hesse, H. (1922). *Siddhartha*. Translated from German by Rosner, H. London: Penguin

Hirvi, J. (2016). *'You Should Know: The First Kidney-Shaped Pool (1939)'*, Transworld Skateboarding, October 2016. Available at: https://skateboarding.transworld.net/features/first-kidney-shaped-pool/#wV38fu7UGoVhoq4F.97

Lothian, K. (2015). *Black Power and the Aboriginal Embassy. Kurrajong*, New South Wales: Subversion Press

Pirsig, R. M. (1974). *Zen and the Art of Motorcycle Maintenance: An Enquiry into Values*. New York: William Morrow and Company

Planet Corroboree (2016). *The Three Brothers*. Planet Corroboree. Available at: https://planetcorroboree.com.au/blogs/culture-country/the-three-brothers

Theroux, P. (1975). *The Old Patagonian Express*. London: Hamish Hamilton

Theroux, P. (1992). *The Happy Isles of Oceania*. London: Hamish Hamilton

Vonnegut, K. (1973). *Breakfast of Champions*. New York: Delacorte Press

Winston, A. (2016). 'Alvar Aalto "Changed the History of Skateboarding"', De Zeen, September 30th 2016. Available at: https://www.dezeen.com/2016/09/30/alvar-aalto-changed-history-skateboarding-villa-mairea-swi mming-pool/

Yugambeh Dreamtime Story in Queensland Parks and Wildlife Service (2009). *Springbrook Nature, Culture and History*. Available at: https://web.archive.org/web/20100324204205/http://www.derm.qld.gov.au/parks/springbrook/culture.html

Gold Coast/Yugambeh: https://www.facebook.com/438629762915824/posts/dreamtime-story-gwyala-dingo-dreamingthis-is-a-dreaming-story-of-a-hunter-gwyala/454885774623556/

https://web.archive.org/web/20100324204205/http://www.derm.qld.gov.au/parks/springbrook/culture.html

Videography

Antihero (2004). *Tent City* (2004). Available at: https://www.youtube.com/watch?v=uXoII5MQqkg&ab_channel=EchoboomSports

Every Hoon Skateboards video (2009 – 2016). Available at: https://www.youtube.com/c/HoonSkateboards/videos and https://www.youtube.com/watch?v=Ho7LWLakNJk&ab_channel=JimsFatHead and https://www.youtube.com/watch?v=zxtRJGGCeHk&ab_channel=ThrasherMagazin

Jackson, P. (1992). *Braindead.*

SKATEPARKS VISITED

Taipei:

Skatepark of Taipei A very BMX/rollerblade heavy design still leaves room for some pretty good lines if you don't mind a jump box or two. I'm sure the vert ramp was great ten years ago, but now it's probably best avoided unless you want to tear your kneecap off on a loose screw.

Queensland:

Brisbane Nundah AKA Flower Street – bowled out miniramp with whiplash transitions, prehistoric pool coping and some exciting cracks and chunks missing, plus a few more recent street course additions.

God Bowl Gnarly pool coping bowl with steps and a death box, as well as a fun little DIY style street course. Located in a Christian centre, so no playing Venom on the speaker system.

Sunshine Coast

Alexandra Heads Amazing bowl with a pool coping deep end and metal coping shallow, with what looked to be a pretty good street set up underneath the three million scooter kids.

Dicky Beach the ugly side of Australian skateparks, with concrete heavily corroded by the sea air and a different kink for every transition in the park; still, I skated it in the dark and accidentally had some sort of fun. I've got a feeling this one might have been replaced with a new park since my visit.

Gold Coast

Pizzey A must if visiting Queensland, the original bowl is legendary and also way gnarlier than it looks on film.

Palm Beach Miniramp Well built six foot miniramp with a channel, but the real draw is the DIY pool coping that local skaters added. Spent a peaceful afternoon there with just the Wu-Tang graffiti for company.

Salk Oval One of the Gold Coast's best; an old dish bowl that has been upgraded with both a DIY doorway/jersey barrier type set up and a brand new skatepark. Pool coping and concrete lips in abundance make for back truck symphony creation.

Tugun One of the area's older and more questionable builds, it has thankfully had a new section tacked on which includes a pretty gnarly, whippy little paint tray bowl.

Nerang A fun miniature peanut bowl alongside a strangely designed bowl, open at one end. A couple of sessions are required to figure out lines, but definitely has potential.

New South Wales:

Ballina A gnarly bowl made no easier by a treacherous paint job, a bank to jersey barrier opposite a bank to curb and a miniramp with three spines, there's plenty of good shit going on in Ballina Skatepark.

Bangalow Rugged pool coping and stairs in the big bowl, tough lines in the small one and a quirky street course make for one of the best stops in the Byron Bay area.
Byron Bay dish – Atomization avoidance zone; 1 in 40 people have been abducted by aliens.

Nimbin The jewel in Northern NSW's skatepark crown. Go there, get scared, gaze in wonderment at where Kevin Kowalski placed his trucks.

Bellingen If outsider art was a skatepark...

Yamba Miniramp extensions, jersey barriers and perfect transitions make for a good day out.

111

Coffs Harbour Newish bowl with flowing lines and a ridiculous vert wall.

Macksville Not from the 1980s, but I'll admit that the miniramp is kind of fun.

Port Macquarie Small, fun bowl and a miniramp you won't get near on a weekend or school holiday. Best off going to skate the DIY sea wall spot and losing your board to the ocean instead.

Newcastle

Islington and Elermore Vale Two ancient, kinked dishes, both clearly built by the same hand and both within 5kms of each other. Noping offers up some crunchy breakfast slashes at either, but Islington just about wins out in gnar factor.

Swansea The forgotten art of the 5 foot miniramp is alive and well in Newcastle's southern suburbs, with Swansea offering one which is bowled out at one end, opens into a street course at the other and has a sub box for good measure.

Bar Beach Frankly terrifying, I mostly stuck to the two shallow pockets. Raven Tershy's shoeless back smith is no joke.

Charlestown There's something off about the big bowl, but the smaller one has plenty of lines. Just don't get collared by dickhead ex cops who want to be friends.

Central Coast

Bateau Bay One of the biggest deep ends in the Southern Hemisphere, but there's fun to be had for the saner skateboarder as well.

Sydney

Five Dock A Sydney institution, with 70s features still intact alongside a huge newer bowl. Lines for days if your legs can hack it.

Manly Vale My favourite kidney bowl in the world, minus the consistent addition by locals of broken glass.

Dulwich Hill – Three eras of skatepark build in one; crusty old snake run with killer DIY additions, badly thought out early 2000s park alongside and a new-ish build with a sick volcano and some Fort Miley-style banks in one corner.

Maroubra Another Sydney favourite, the rolling banks of the street course were overrun with kids so I stuck to the bowl, which was great in spite of the burnt out holes in the flat bottom of the deep.

Sydenham Green One of the city's newest, incorporates an incredible street course with a slightly off, but still enjoyable, kidney.

Galston Almost a DIY spot of a skatepark built around a rough as guts pool, this one took a few long necks to loosen the legs. Highly recommended if you find yourself deep in the Northern Suburbs and in need of a scare.

French's Forest vert ramp A ten foot vert ramp is ideal when you're too intimidated to skate modern monstrosities. Been around for years, but recently resurfaced and stripped of its channel gap.

Sydney to Vic

Albury As mentioned above, a ten foot vert ramp is ideal; the exception being one that's about ten feet wide. A sheet metal deathtrap which I had no intention of skating without some crew to fire things up, garnished with a bizarre concrete bowl/street layout featuring six inch high handrails and kinked, cracked transitions which were pretty much flatbanks. Honourable mention goes to the foot high vert quarterpipe.

Holbrook Who gives a fuck about the shitty skatepark, there's a grounded submarine just across the road!

Australian Capital Territory

Belconnen As legendary as Pizzey or Corio, the new bit kind of sucks but the keyhole will keep you busy enough to forget about anything else. Anything you've seen done across the channel is fucking gnarly.

The Yard Canberra's secret gem, with a space that should be too cramped for the amount of obstacles involved ending up being loads of fun.

Victoria

Benalla An old rusty metal reminder of the bad days of skatepark building, thankfully next to a pretty new bowl with some satisfying lines despite it's clearly BMX heavy design.

Corio 80s cheese grating terror. Choose your own adventure with either the keyhole or the paint tray, both are out for blood.

Torquay Would be great if it wasn't so fucking slippery. Fuck overly sealed concrete.

Whittlesea Miniramp Looks great on photos, but in actual fact makes no sense and was clearly built by people with only the vaguest idea of what a skateboard, let alone a skatepark, looks like. Kinks, cracks and a number of badly thought out extensions (including a 'snake run' from the platform at one end) make it a worthwhile novelty for the curious.

Daylesford Some of the freshest concrete I skated in VIC, loads of fun and a dope camping spot to boot.

Ballarat The second largest town in VIC boasts a concrete park with a bunch of interesting obstacles and lines, as well as some next level street spots.

Ararat Well designed bowl with questionable 90s style street course appendage.

Horsham One of the pleasures of Australia is finding skateparks you'd love as a local in the arse end of nowhere. Horsham is halfway between Melbourne and the Victoria/South Australia border, above the Grampian Range, and boasts a ridiculously good park for a town of its size.

Melbourne Northern Suburbs

Greensborough Half forgotten concrete savagery in the depths of Melbourne's north – Cuzza kills it in 'Hoon Run – The Movie'.

Epping Similarly gnarly and similarly visible getting wrecked in various Hoon videos, it also has plenty of smaller transitions and obstacles to satisfy most tastes.

Fawkner A lesson in how to build small scale skateparks, Fawkner is one of the Northern Suburbs' most regularly sessioned spots.

Coburg The best bowl in Melbourne hands down, I'll fight any cunt who says different. Leaks in the winter, gets bins burnt in it in the summer, the flat bottom is basically gravel and the transitions have vert nearly all the way around. Could only be better with pool coping, and I've heard that there have been talks with the council about that happening.

Reservoir One of the most unique skatepark designs I've seen on my travel, including a Melbourne tram barrier replica, a smattering of jersey barriers that are harder to skate than some legit 'street' ones I've visited, and every kind of ledge you can imagine. The closest a skatepark can come to being a street spot.

Keon A metal miniramp with an accidentally oververt extension; this was updated recently with a tiny alleyway of a street course which features a great bank to curb, but the tetanus bit is still the main draw.

Brunswick Lots of controversy around this one, apparently the locals wanted a more street style layout but instead they got a clover bowl with an 11 foot vert deep end. The sun shuts it down for an hour or two in the late afternoon (depending on what time of year it is), but this is made up for by the gaps cut in the metal coping, offering an authentic faux pool coping feel. Glenroy – Pretty sure it would be fun if the local community didn't use it as a creche.

Fitzroy Unassuming looking bowls which somehow became an essential part of the Melbourne skateboarding experience. Fun to skate for an hour or two, fun to drink on the benches for way longer.

Northcote Not sure who designed this one, the lines only half work and there are some deadly kinks in the bowl but, despite this, it somehow always delivered the goods when the session got fired up.

Bulleen Possibly the oldest skatepark in Melbourne, a badly designed snake run was pimped out a few years ago with an actual deep end and a few curbs and jersey barriers to make it properly skateable.

Melbourne Western Suburbs

Newport Like Brunswick, the coping in the bowl has been cut for an extra depth of sound, but the overall build quality is nowhere near as good. Still worth a visit if in the area, if only for the novelty of powering through frontside grinds whilst in the background ships glide up the Yarra River.

Kensington Rumour has it this is Tony Trujillo's favourite miniramp in Australia; a six foot spine ramp with a pump bump and enough length to lock in a grind for as long as you like, I can see why.

Yarraville An absolute mess where every obstacle is potentially a rolled ankle.

Ring of Fire Melbourne is pretty short on indoor parks, but this one more than makes up for that as long as you take a broom and some fizzy pop to throw over the transitions and damp down the dust. Large bowl with a vert wall and pool coping corners tucked away in the loft of a bizarre funhouse/static carnie site.

Sunshine Plaza CURBS!!!

Sunshine West Bog standard street course elevated to visit-worthy levels by a whippy miniramp with a pretty savage extension.

Hopper's Crossing A fair way south from Melbourne's CDB lies one of the fastest bowls in the Metropolitan area. Loads of lines to be found here, and when your legs give out there's a foot high spine to piss around on.

Point Cook One of the various sacrificial pits designed by Dorfus, this one makes for a good double hit with Hopper's Crossing and is equal parts intimidating and incredible.

Deer Park One of Melbourne's forgotten skateparks, this one is of questionable build quality but a session can still get going once you've mapped out the burnt out holes on the flat bottom.

Central Melbourne

Riverslide Loads of fun obstacles, but good luck getting a session quiet enough to enjoy them all.

St Kilda Some of the best pool coping in the city, endless lines in the bowl, but as with Riverslide can get pretty swamped.

Melbourne Eastern Suburbs

Elwood Old crust pits lying just down the road from St Kilda; worth visiting when the low lying sun takes out half of that park until dusk, just don't go expecting skatepark quality building.

Clayton Bowled out miniramp with a pool coping extension, tucked away in the arse end of the Eastern Suburbs but worth checking out if you find yourself down that way.

Sandringham Like a good version of Elwood, but with just one rather than two bowls and less of a street course.

Knox Out towards the Dandenongs lies one of the best parks in the city; two bowls, one with a cradle and one small but whippy beast, garnished with transitions of varying steepness around the outside. Don't sleep on this one if you have a car.

Old Knox Fitzroy's deformed older brother also features a crumbling snake run and a rusty metal miniramp. A predilection for crust is necessary to enjoy this one.

Noble One of Melbourne's biggest and best, but the twelve foot deep end puts the shits up me.

Box Hill A combination of new and old park, not as well thought out as Knox or Noble but does have lights and is a little closer to the city than Noble.

Tasmania

West Hobart Snake Run OG crust spot which has seen visits from a number of skateboarding luminaries over the years...sadly wet when we visited, but looks as hard to skate as you'd expect it to be.

South Hobart Good sized (7 foot-ish) miniramp, alongside a basic but fun concrete park layout. Kangaroo Bay – Huge kidney pool and flowing street course, this one offers a more modern layout than either West or South Hobart skateparks.

Launceston Abstract crust including haggard concrete

midiramp, large tarmac roll in and gnarly vert wall on top of a bank.

<u>New Zealand:</u>

South Island

Queenstown Gardens A big, gnarly fucker of a bowl and a street course with a whole corner dedicated to jersey barriers? Yes please.

Wanaka Not quite as good a bowl as Queenstown Gardens down the road, but way deeper for those partial to a vert session. The old bowl and the park surrounding it aren't all that, but the combination of big transition, pool coping and scenery is hard to beat.

Dunedin Small and steep with the occasional DIY vert wall to spice things up, this one's not winning any beauty contests but it's fun enough if you're in the area.

Mornington Skatepark AKA The Blood Bucket As far as I know the oldest skatepark on the South Island, this one is as gnarly as its name would have you believe; minimal flat bottom, a roll in which in no way helps with speed and a weathered concrete lip, I waited for three days for it to dry up and it was worth every penny I spent sitting in bars for that time. The hillbomb back into the city is an added bonus.

Washington Way, Christchurch Has pretty much everything you could want in a skatepark, I could have spent weeks there and still been finding new lines.

Waltham Bowl Looked like good, crusty fun, but the deep end had been filled with tree branches and flooded, so we just tramlined a miniramp session in the shallow end.

Picton Weathered bumps, strange indents in the floor, an eight foot midiramp with angle iron coping...not really sure what was going on here, but I think I liked it

119

Nelson As head scratching as Picton, the tiny kidney bowl seemed to be cobbled together from ten different skatepark plans.

North Island

Waitangi Park One of the best bowls on either island, this one plays host to Wellington Bowl-O-Rama every year for good reason.

Palmerston North Clocked up twelve staples in the back of my head, so it must have been good.

Melville Bowl In the middle of a refurb, so I may never know. Cheers to Acid Skateparks for the tour of the building site, it seemed as if it was going to be a good one!

New Lynn Built in centimetres rather than the desired inches, or some similar result of miscommunication, means a claustrophobic ride down the snake run. Apparently it was rougher before a renovation a few years ago, but is definitely still no slouch on the crust front. Legendarily dumb.

Victoria Park Just plain dumb; some of the street obstacles aren't bad, but this one's best avoided if you want a good transition hit.

Lynfield Some concrete feels harder than most, and Lynfield is fucking nails. A must visit if in Auckland.